Regent's Study Guides

General Editor: Paul S. Fiddes

OLD TESTAMENT PICTURES OF GOD

REGENT'S STUDY GUIDES

OLD TESTAMENT PICTURES OF GOD

Rex Mason

Regent's Park College
Oxford

with

Smyth and Helwys Publishing, Inc.
Macon, Georgia

for Audrey

ISBN 0 9518104 1 3 (UK)
ISBN 1-880837-33-1 (USA)

OLD TESTAMENT PICTURES OF GOD
Copyright © 1993
Published by Regent's Park College, Oxford OX1 2LB UK
in association with Smyth & Helwys Publishing, Inc.,
Macon, Georgia 31207 USA
All rights reserved
Printed in the United States of America

The paper used in this publication meets the minimum requirements of American National Standard for Information Sciences—Permanence of Paper for Printed Library Materials, ANSI Z39.48-1984.

CONTENTS

ABBREVIATIONS AND ACKNOWLEDGEMENT vi

INTRODUCTION 1

1. GOD AS REDEEMER 17

2. GOD AS CRAFTSMAN 31

3. GOD AS FATHER 45

4. GOD AS HUMAN 75

5. GOD AS KING 91

6. GOD AS JUDGE 123

7. GOD AS SHEPHERD 143

8. GOD AS WARRIOR 159

9. GOD AS LOVER 175

10. GOD AS FEMININE 189

CONCLUSION 205

INDEX 207

ABBREVIATIONS

JB	The Jerusalem Bible
LXX	The Septuagint (Greek version of the Old Testament)
NEB	The New English Bible
RSV	The Revised Standard Version

ACKNOWLEDGEMENT

Except where otherwise stated, the translations of the Old and New Testament texts used in this book are all from The Revised Standard Version, and are used by kind permission of the Division of Christian Education of the National Council of the Churches of Christ in the United States of America.

INTRODUCTION

There is an Indian story of four blind men who were sitting by the roadside when an elephant passed by. Intrigued by the sound—and possibly alerted by other senses—they wondered what it might be. 'The first felt a leg, and said it was a tree; the second an ear, and said it was a basket; the third its tusks, and said it was a plough; the fourth its trunk, and was sure it was a snake.'[1] Each comparison was quite lively and imaginative and expressed vividly some aspect of that slightly odd but extremely useful wonder of creation, the elephant. Taken by itself, however, each picture was misleading. It is hardly surprising that the whole truth about an elephant should be greater than the sum of its parts.

Blind men trying to grasp and express the whole truth about an elephant may not be a wholly inappropriate analogy for the task which faces us as human beings when we try to grasp the nature of God and to express it. That nature must, by definition, be something unfamiliar to and larger than the normal concepts our minds are used to grasping and formulating. Here, we are all 'blind men' for, 'No one has ever seen God' (John 1: 18). Yet many people claim that he is not totally unknowable. Men and women in all ages and among many communities of faith tell us that they have caught a rustle of his garment as he passes by. They believe he has left signs of his presence by which they have known him and experienced relationship with him. Yet the problem has always been how adequately to describe him.

From an early stage in the journey of Christian thought some have said that, since God must be different from human beings, the only safe way of talking about him is to say what he is *not*. This has been known as the *via negativa*, describing God by negatives. So the classical theological terms applied to God have often been negatives. He cannot be limited by our finite human nature, so he is Infinite. He cannot be conditioned by human emotions, so he must be Impassible. He cannot consist of created matter, so he is Incorporeal. He cannot be described adequately in any language, so he is Ineffable. To continue to describe God only by what he is not, however, is, eventually, to lose sight of him altogether from any real kind of human knowledge. Gradually he fades from human view like the Cheshire Cat in *Alice in Wonderland,* leaving only a general impression of vague beneficence behind him:

> This time it vanished quite slowly, beginning with the end of the tail, and ending with the grin, which remained some time after the rest of it had gone.[2]

If God, in effect, is only utterly and essentially different from everything human and everything the human mind can conceive, it is difficult to see how we can know anything of him at all. As John Macquarrie says:

> If one adhered strictly to the *via negationis*, it is hard to see how the knowledge of God reached in this way could be other than wholly vacuous. It would scarcely be distinguishable from agnosticism, and while indeed . . . a measure of reverent agnosticism is entirely proper in any discourse that respects the mystery and uniqueness of God, faith is possible only on the basis that God has granted some positive knowledge of himself.[3]

The people of Israel were much bolder in their approach. They made use of a whole range of 'picture' language to speak about God. Their Scriptures, which Jews know as TANAK[4] and Christians as 'The Old Testament' are like an art gallery on whose walls are exhibited a rich variety of pictures of God. It is remarkable that a people who were forbidden (officially, at least) to make any visual image of God (Exod. 20: 4 cf. Deut. 5: 8) yet produced this array of literary images. The Old Testament talk about God abounds in simile and metaphor.[5] Not all the pictures are unique to Israel. Some of them, as we shall see, were the common stock of the people among whom Israel lived in the Ancient Near East. From them she received much in her culture, religion and national life. Yet the use she made of these images and the rich and multi-coloured tapestry she produced from them in her scriptures are unique and have become part of the devotional heritage of three major world religions, Judaism, Christianity and Islam.

It is the purpose of this book to examine some of the main pictures of God drawn in the Old Testament and the use which is made of them there. Such a study is bound to raise the very far-reaching question, 'Can the use of such pictures to talk about God be justified?' There is an old joke which says, 'In the beginning God created man in his own image—and ever since man has been repaying him the compliment'! Theologians tend to talk with lips pursed anxiously about 'anthropomorphism'. It comes from two Greek words, one meaning 'man' or 'human' and the other 'form' or 'shape'. 'Anthropomorphism' therefore means talking about God in human terms or 'as if he were a human being'. This has often been seen as either a very primitive and naive way of talking about God, or as downright heresy. Often, it has been viewed as both! To speak so of God, who must be bigger than and different from the merely human, is to limit him. It is to reduce him to our own size and weakness, an image of our own creation. As such, it is claimed, it is a form of idolatry.

These are grave charges. Can we defend the Old Testament use of pictures to describe God, pictures mostly drawn from human life and experience, against such advocacy in the court of theology and hope to get an acquittal? There are at least some points a good Counsel for the Defence could and should make before the verdict of guilty is pronounced and sentence passed.

The first is that, whenever we want to speak about something beyond our present knowledge and experience, we have to start from that which we do know. The language of simile, metaphor, symbol and analogy[6] is indispensable, and that is why they have been described as the 'life-blood' of poetry. By them a poet can enlarge the horizons of our mind, imagination and experience. So G.B. Caird says:

> Comparison is one of our most valuable sources of knowledge, the main road leading from the known to the unknown. It comprises a large part of our daily speech *and almost all the language of theology*. God speaks to man in similitudes (Hos.

12: 10), and man has no language but analogy for speaking about God, however inadequate it may be.[7]

We need not apologise for using pictures in talking about God, then, even if we must exercise caution in doing so. Simile, and like expressions, are the necessary visa for travelling from the known to the unknown. Without this visa no adventurer after God will be admitted to the kingdom. Indeed, the very term 'kingdom' which he uses to describe the object of his journey, is itself a simile.

The second point to be made about the picture language for God in the Old Testament is that it is extremely *personal*. The great majority of pictures are drawn from the realm of human relationships, the relationships between *persons*. To call God 'Father', 'King', 'Lover', 'Redeemer', 'Shepherd', 'Craftsman', 'Warrior' and so on, is to find in human relationships something of the nature of God. Even when inanimate pictures are used, like 'the Rock', it is still the aspect of those objects as experienced by human beings, such as strength and reliability, which is being stressed. Behind this lies a profound theological affirmation. It is the faith of the Priestly Writer[8] of the Babylonian exile, from whom comes the account of creation to be found in Gen. 1:1-2:4a, that people are made 'in the image of God':

> So God created man in his own image, in the image of God he created him; male and female he created them. (Gen. 1: 27).

Whatever that means, its meaning must include the recognition that there is some 'point of contact' between God and human beings, whatever vast differences soar like mountain ranges between them. Our 'humanity' is a sphere in which God is already revealing himself. 'Personality' is an attribute shared by Creator and creature. Relationships between people open a door to an awareness of relationship with God. Indeed, they already are a real if, as yet, unrecognised relationship with God through relationship with his creatures.

This seems to bring us closest to some of the things being said by 'existentialist' theologians. John Macquarrie speaks of the relationship between human and divine in the following terms:

> Such symbolism [he is speaking of the symbolism of the Incarnation] is possible because every particular being has its participation in Being and so to some extent manifests and illuminates Being . . .[9]

It is revealing that the Old Testament in general does not start from certain abstract doctrines about God. To some extent God is 'deduced' from human experience, from the events of history and the world of creation. It is the conviction of prophets, priests and law-givers that he speaks to people in 'many and various ways' as the writer of the Letter to the Hebrews puts it (Heb. 1:1). It is no coincidence, therefore, that it is the Old Testament, to an extent unique in ancient religious literature, which rifles the stockpile of metaphor provided by human relationships in its attempts to describe God and human experience of him.

Further, it should be noted that the boldness and verve of the Old Testament writers in their use of such picture language about God are in no way embarrassed by anything like the more extreme versions of the Christian doctrine of the 'Fall'. Christian readers who find in Genesis chapter 3 a doctrine of an original fall of humankind which has resulted in a lasting and total depravity find this, not so much in Genesis, as in the exegetical traditions which some Christians have erected on it. One of the most prominent and influential examples of these is Milton's epic poem, *Paradise Lost*. The Old Testament writers are fully realistic about human sinfulness, to be sure. But one searches the Old Testament in vain for anything equivalent to some Christian traditions of the Fall, that depict people as having become so utterly depraved that the 'image' of God in them has been distorted to the point where no possible point of contact between the human and the divine remains. All the main Old Testament traditions believe that God takes the initiative in any revelation of himself and all see that initiative as the expression of his grace. But they believe that even sinful people are capable of recognising his grace for what it is and responding to it, for God is already present in their life and in their relationships.

Perhaps it is not surprising that it was some of the severer forms of Puritanism which put their energies into defacing and removing what they saw as 'images'. Their theology made them suspicious of the capacity of any sense of human beauty and wonder about God and his creation to be a true expression of God and to lead to experience of God. Even the rich verbal 'imagery' of the Old Testament writers could never have flourished under them, although they were more indebted to it than they realised or allowed. The portrait gallery provided by the Old Testament writers in which so many pictures of God in human terms are displayed side by side, has very significant theological overtones indeed. The suspicions about anthropomorphism are difficult to sustain if we believe that human nature itself is an expression of the divine. Christians especially, believe that God has made the supreme revelation of himself in a human life, that of Jesus of Nazareth.

A third point for the defence of these human pictures to speak about God springs from the reflection that they have proved to be very powerful and creative. One has only to think of the influence Psalm 23 has exerted on generations of the Jewish and Christian communities of faith, expressed not least for the Christian church in the hymn, 'The Lord's My Shepherd'. Partly, as we have already argued, this is due to the power of poetry, with its figures of speech and symbols, to evoke a 'feeling' of the truth of what may other-wise be merely notional, intellectual belief. Partly, it is because of the deep underlying conception that our human relationships and experience are part of the divine life and activity by which God gives himself to the creatures he has made in his own image. Thus all such pictures have an 'existential' force. They are revelation of the reality at the heart of all human life and experience. They are not merely informative: they call for response. If I believe that God is 'Father' I am faced with the question of whether I trust him and obey him as a son. If I believe that God is 'Judge', I have to ask whether I am prepared to submit character, motives, deeds, and also my inaction, to the blazing judgement of his holiness. If I believe that, in any sense, he is 'Lover', I have to recall that love calls for love.

Not surprisingly, it is John Macquarrie who reminds us of this. Comparing the use of metaphor and symbol in poetry with religious discourse, he argues that, whereas in poetry they play an aesthetic role, 'the religious symbol, analogue or image calls from us a response of commitment'.[10] This is certainly how the Old Testament writers, especially the prophets, used symbols.

INTRODUCTION

Typical of this call for response is the question Malachi portrays God as asking of his people:

> A son honours his father
> and a servant his master.
> If then I am a father,
> Where is my honour? (Mal. 1: 6).

Macquarrie is right to see this continuing into the New Testament:

> ... when we think of some of the images that were applied by the first Christians to Christ, these involved a faith-commitment to him. To call him 'Lord', or 'Son of God' ... is not so much to light up his being ... as to respond to him by accepting him and declaring one's allegiance to him or obedience to him.[11]

This brings us to the heart of what the communities of faith claim is the only way to 'know' God. We must, indeed, know something about him if we are to respond at all. But only by an 'existential' faith-commitment do I, as a person, come to know God in any kind of 'personal' relationship. It is in their function, not only as 'informers', but as 'summoners to faith' and as nourishment for the devotional life of relationship with God that the pictures have proved their value.

Nevertheless, we have to listen very carefully to the warnings sounded by Christian theologians as well as to the cautionary notes sounded in the Old Testament itself. Even in the case of a human being, no portrait, however 'life-like', captures the living, flesh and blood, three dimensional appearance and complex personality of the original in anything but faint outline and conventional form. Further, subjective and interpretative elements always creep in. We have only to compare different portraits of the same sitter by different painters to realise how various artists 'see' the original differently. Each detects some aspects of appearance, character and personality, but any human being is so complex that it is difficult to say which is the 'truer' likeness. If this is so of human beings how much more must it be true, by definition, of God.

No one 'picture' could correspond exactly or completely to the reality we call 'God'. He must be too big to be caged and domesticated entirely in our human concepts and experience. That is why, at the very least, we need many pictures, each filling out a little the imperfections and incompleteness of others. To think of God only as 'Lover' might easily lead to a flabby and sickly sentimentality unless we also think of him as 'Judge'.

To think of him as 'Father' might lead us to domesticate God unless we also thought of him as universal 'King'. To depict him only as 'Warrior' might lead to the concept of a God of iron and blood. To remember that he can also be portrayed as 'Shepherd' brings another dimension to our awareness. In our opening story, each Indian was 'wrong' in his identification of his bit of the elephant. Even taken together their descriptions would leave us with the impression of a rather odd creature! But with all four pictures we might well be a little less wrong than we should otherwise have been. God must remain a mystery to us. Yet to say that, and admit that all our pictures are partial, is one thing. To say that we know nothing of him is quite another. In these pictures we may see *something*, even if only 'as through a glass darkly' and not yet 'face to face' (1 Cor. 13: 12).

From this stems another limitation on our use of these Old Testament pictures of God or, indeed, of any other pictures. We cannot use them as staging posts from which to journey on to claim that they 'prove' the existence of God. We cannot employ them in any kind of 'ontological' argument, to use the traditional theological term. A popular and over-simplified version of this argument has become widely current in the following form. We humans have the idea of 'Fatherhood'. Indeed, we can conceive of the idea of perfect fatherhood even although we never encounter such an abstract thing on earth. Since God must be 'that than which no greater can be conceived', there must be somewhere some objective reality which does express perfect fatherhood to which our ideas correspond and of which they are an expression. Such 'perfection' must, by definition, be 'God'. This, however, cannot stand as a proof. It is one thing to say that, if God exists and if he is personal, then we may expect to find something of him in our existence as persons and in our relationships with other persons. To argue the other way round and to say that, because we are persons and know these kinds of relationships, there must be a God like this, is not only to attempt an unwarranted logical leap over too wide a chasm, but to run the grave risk of 'deifying' our own thoughts and experience. It really is to break the second commandment forbidding the making of 'images' and calling them 'God'.

Those who belong to the communities of faith will want to affirm that God is not known by 'proof' anyway. He is known by experience and in 'relationship'. He comes to us in grace and self-disclosure; we respond to him in faith. That is the starting-point for all religious experience. But the need to describe the God whom they believe comes to them is important both in communicating the nature of the community's faith and in sharpening its hold on mind and life. The descriptions of God which come from Old and New Testaments are themselves objective witness to the nature of that faith in the tradition. In them we hear the heartbeat of faith and may feel the pulse of experience.

．．．．．．．．．．．．．．．．．．．．

Perhaps a word, if not of apology, at least of explanation, is due, because the theme of this book is that of 'Old Testament Pictures of God.' Such a treatment might expose flanks to two lines of cross-fire.

To talk of the 'Old Testament' as a whole may sound as naive as the evangelist who, in the heat and enthusiasm of the moment, proclaims what *the Bible* says'. The Bible clearly speaks with varied voices which say different things. Have not decades of critical biblical scholarship shown that the 'Old Testament' is an amalgam of many different sources and traditions? It has become evident that almost any book within it represents the final deposit of a long process of growth and development in which many hands have played a shaping part and varied traditions have found voice. Exegetes and interpreters have re-interpreted in new situations things said long before. As we catch a glimpse of the way the books have grown, we discover the way that the 'Word of God' has been heard in one generation by the community of God's people, and then its relevance has been applied, and new meaning has been found within it, as new challenges have come in future years. As we study the Old Testament and enter into this process of the preaching and the re-preaching of the word of God, we are enabled to hear God's word for our own time.

So we must always defend these gains of understanding that have been achieved. It has been the strength of critical scholarship to show that the Old Testament is not a seamless garment, but a rich coat of many colours. The Deuteronomists (those who were responsible for the final form of Deuteronomy, Joshua-II Kings and the Book of Jeremiah, as well as interpretative comments in several other books), the Chronicler and the 'Priestly Writer' (see note 8) all interpret Israel's history from different points of view and with widely varying theological aims. There are great differences between pre-exilic prophets and the prophets who spoke during and after the exile, and between all of these and the so-called 'cultic prophets' who functioned at sanctuaries and probably played a large part in the production and earliest use of the Psalms. The 'Wisdom' writers, who produced Proverbs and the books of Job and Ecclesiastes and contributed to many other Old Testament books, have their own presuppositions, purposes and theological approach, all of which exhibit significant differences even among themselves. Those who produced the so-called 'Apocalyptic Literature' (Dan., Joel, Isa. 24-27, Zech. 9-14 are all marked to a greater or lesser extent by some of the characteristics often described as 'Apocalyptic') interpret God's action in history differently from the prophets.

There is nothing to be gained, and a great deal to be lost, by either ignoring these differences or attempting to smooth them down by some exegetical honing into one edgeless (and lifeless) whole. We can listen to those who in recent years have been urging us to take the final 'canonical' form of the Hebrew scriptures seriously rather than merely fragmenting the text into many disparate pieces by analytical methods.[12] But we have to insist that we can only hear the symphonic effects of the final score if we examine the individual instrumental parts, each of which is an indispensable component of the resulting sound. This has its tonal richness only because of the many sounds which comprise it and the counterpoint which gives depth to the harmony.

We shall, therefore, be alert to differences in the way these pictures are used (or, indeed, are not used) in the different traditions that comprise the Old Testament. What we can hardly hope to do with any confidence is to claim to be able to construct some kind of historical 'development' in the use of these pictures and the meaning given to them. Not only are we often still uncertain of the date of various books and sources within those books in spite of all our critical investigations, but even in a source claimed with some confidence to belong to a specific period (e.g. Deuteronomy to the 7th. century BCE), we cannot be sure how far it may be utilising older and more traditional concepts, even deliberately archaizing them, or, on the other hand, re-interpreting them by giving them a new 'twist' in the contemporary situation. We must be very cautious, then, over claims, more often heard in the past, to trace a 'development' in Israel's religious ideas. Developments there obviously were, but we cannot chart them with precision. Often, different views of varying religious depth and value co-existed side by side, as they do still in any religious community. Religious ideas do not always evolve from the 'lesser' to the 'greater'. Saintliness and superstition are often near neighbours in any religious community.

The fact remains, however, that if the Old Testament is a coat of many colours, it is still a coat which has protected the whole continuing community of Judaism. It has been also the main watershed where the river of Christianity has its source. There is, then, value in trying to view the use of these pictures across the whole spectrum of Old Testament witness. Both the unity and diversity of the Old Testament are real parts of its rich legacy.[13]

The other flank which a study of 'Old Testament Pictures of God' might seem to expose could well be vulnerable to attack from Christians. Why limit such a study to the Old Testament? Some might go farther. Since it is the New Testament which contains explicit witness to Jesus Christ, why bother with the Old Testament at all? An immediate answer is that there is no real understanding of the New Testament without the Old, and this is one reason why it has always been the sure instinct of the Christian church to insist, against all assaults, that the Old Testament is part of the Canon of Scripture. It was the Bible of Jesus, of the first disciples and of all the writers of the New Testament. Its language, thought and symbolism were the elements of their natural soil. At the least, therefore, it provides us with an indispensable key for unlocking the doors to understanding of the New Testament. Yet Christians must always beware of reading the Old Testament only in the light of the New. If we use it only as a sounding board to bounce back to ourselves ideas we bring to it from the New, not only do we deny that the Old Testament is a valid word of God in itself, but we lose the light it has to shed on the New. We shine the beam in one direction only and consequently much remains obscure. The way these pictures are taken up in the New Testament, both in continuity and discontinuity, is a fascinating and important study. But that study, like all study of the New Testament, must be based on a strong foundation of real understanding of what the Old Testament was saying.

Both because these pictures have nourished the faith of Judaism, and because that light was passed through the new prism of Jesus and of Christian interpretation of his person and work, the study of Old Testament symbolism remains a valid and necessary undertaking. To recover its true force, to be sure, takes a little time and patience. The pictures in the Old Testament portrait gallery need a little cleaning and restoration if we are to see them with the freshness and vividness of colour they had for those who first used them. 'Shepherds' and 'Redeemers' are not part of everyday experience in our modern, urban culture. Yet, just because they deal for the most part with human relationships and the pigments they use are drawn from the colour box of human experience, they still have power and vitality to reach across the centuries and speak to us directly and simply.

....

Old Testament scholars will recognise soon enough that this book is not intended for them. It is intended not, perhaps, for the passenger in the Clapham omnibus (a classic English way of describing 'the ordinary man or woman', since Clapham is not considered one of the more exotic parts of London), but for an adventurous lay person in the pew. To save such people the forbidding task of hacking their way through a dense undergrowth of endnotes these have been kept to a minimum. Where they do occur they usually refer readers to books they might have a chance of finding in a public library, at least in one with helpful staff! Technical terms, where they have to be used, are explained. It may be that, for this reason, the work of individual scholars is not acknowledged as it ought to be. I hope they will take this general expression of my indebtedness and gratitude.

What may strike the pewperson as unfamiliar are the references to, and quotations from, some of the literature of Israel's neighbours in the Ancient Near East. These peoples did not produce anything like our Old Testament, and there do not appear to have grown among them widespread communities of faith who collected their sacred writings and came to view them as possessing canonical authority for their beliefs. Nevertheless, almost every kind of book and writing in the Old Testament has its parallels among Israel's neighbours. It is important to see that their thought neither developed in an intellectual or religious vacuum, nor slavishly copied the beliefs and thoughts of others without re-minting them. We can only appreciate Israel's 'uniqueness' when we have first seen her indebtedness. That is why, when we examine some of the 'pictures of God' which were widespread in the ancient world, I include some of the comparative material. But the sections in which this is done can easily be skipped by those who find it all too forbidding!

....

In this introductory chapter I have tried to prepare for some of the difficulties we are likely to meet later on our journey of investigation of the Old Testament pictures of God. How can we speak of God at all? How valid are pictures drawn from human relationships and experience in our attempts to speak of him? Why should the Old Testament be thought to have any kind of unified or cogent voice? Why should we choose the Old Testament for our itinerary anyway? We have seen that there are dangers and limitations of which we must be wary on the way. But we have seen also that there are good reasons for undertaking the journey and signs which provide real hope that we shall make discoveries on the way and at its end. It is fitting that we should turn to a prophet of the Old Testament for a word to conclude this part of our discussion and prepare us for what is to follow. He is the prophet of the Babylonian exile (597-538 BCE) who is often called the 'Second Isaiah'.[14] He cites God as saying,

> To whom will you liken me and make me equal,
> and compare me, that we may be alike? (Isa. 46: 5).

By recording God as asking that question he thus warns us of the dangers inherent in our enterprise. But this same prophet also says:

> For your Maker is your husband,
> the LORD of Hosts is his name;
> and the Holy One of Israel is your Redeemer,
> the God of the whole earth he is called. (Isa. 54: 5)

By thus himself using pictures which liken God to husband and kinsman he encourages us to undertake the enquiry. If such picture language could nourish the faith of exiled Israel at the zero-point of their fortunes it may well nourish ours. We must heed the risks. Equally, we must be ready for the rewards.

NOTES TO THE INTRODUCTION

1. The quotation is from C.R. North, *The Suffering Servant in Deutero-Isaiah*, Oxford, 1948, p.111. He uses the story to illustrate its application to the many theories about the identity of the 'Servant' in Isaiah chapters 40-55, and attributes its first use in this context to Wilhelm Fischer.

2. Lewis Carroll, *Alice's Adventures in Wonderland* (1865), in the chapter called 'Pig and Pepper'.

3. J. Macquarrie, *God Talk*, London, 1967, pp.26f.

4. The name *TANAK* is formed from the initial letters of the three main sections of the Canon of the Jewish Scriptures. These are: *Torah* (Law, i.e. the Pentateuch, the first five books), *Nᵉbi'im* (Prophets, comprising the 'former prophets', i.e. the history books from Joshua–II Kings, and

INTRODUCTION 15

the 'latter prophets', i.e. Isaiah, Jeremiah, Ezekiel and 'The Book of the Twelve') and *Kᵉthûbîm*, the 'Writings', comprising all the other books.

5. For the way in which these terms are used in this book, see n. 6 below.

6. These terms are being used quite generally here and, since the argument does not depend upon the distinguishing of one from the other, the exact semantic range of each is not sought by definition. In general terms 'simile' is used to say that one thing is *like* another, as in the line, 'My love is like a red, red rose'. Metaphor is a 'compressed' simile, by which something is said to *be* the other thing with which it is compared, as in Shakespeare's rather delightful use of 'mixed' metaphor in Hamlet's soliloquy:

> 'Whether 'tis nobler in the mind to suffer
> The slings and arrows of outrageous fortune,
> Or to take arms against a sea of troubles,
> And by opposing end them?'

'Symbol' indicates the use of one thing to express a meaning, or range of meanings, beyond itself. This may be quite arbitrary as in the use of a red traffic light to indicate a command to stop. Or something may be seen to be symbolic by virtue of the properties inherent within it. So 'water' is a powerful symbol in religious thought because it can symbolise cleansing, refreshment, life or power. 'Analogy' makes use of the fact that one, or more, principles which operate in a given realm, may operate also in another. The writer of the First Letter to Peter uses an argument by analogy when, counselling his readers to nourish and develop their life of the spirit, he says, 'Like the new-born infants you are, you must crave for pure milk (spiritual milk, I mean), so that you may thrive upon it to your souls' health' (I Pet. 2: 2, NEB). This goes beyond simile because it assumes that principles similar to those governing physical development, govern, by analogy, spiritual development as well. It is clear that the semantic boundaries between these terms are blurred, with quite a large area of overlap. There are wide tracts of common land between them.

7. G.B. Caird, *The Language and Imagery of the Bible*, London, 1980. The italics are mine.

8. For over a century it has been the view of most Old Testament scholars that the first five books of the Bible, the 'Pentateuch' (from the Greek, meaning 'five-fold scroll') is made up of a number of different layers or sources, dating from the 10th. to the 5th. centuries BCE and that these have been edited to form our present Pentateuch over a long period. The latest of these, dating from the time of the Babylonian exile and beyond, is called the 'Priestly Code' or 'Priestly Writing' because it shows great interest in matters of worship, sacrificial ritual, priesthood and sacral law and has a very distinctive literary style. It is usually held to represent plans by priestly writers in exile for life in Israel after their return from Babylon. Much in it may be either earlier or later than this time, however. Other 'sources' in the Pentateuch will be discussed when they are mentioned in the text.

9. *God Talk*, p.145

10. *God Talk*, p.195

11. *Ibid*.

12. See, e.g. B.S. Childs, *Introduction to the Old Testament as Scripture*, London, 1979.

13. A recent treatment of the value of unity and diversity as seen within the Old Testament is found in John Goldingay's *Theological Diversity and the Authority of the Old Testament*, Grand Rapids, Michigan, 1987. An earlier study which represented a similar approach to the New Testament was James Dunn's, *Unity and Diversity in the New Testament*, London, 1970.

14. It has long been recognised that chs. 40-55 are from a different author than the writer of much that is found in Isa. chs. 1-39. Chs. 1-39 are substantially from the eighth century prophet, Isaiah, often called 'Isaiah of Jerusalem' to distinguish him from the author of chs. 40-55. This latter author was an unknown prophet who ministered towards the end of the time of the Babylonian exile, encouraging the exiles by assuring them that God was about to enable them to return to their homeland.

I

GOD AS REDEEMER

Many Christians will be so accustomed to using the term 'Redeemer' of Jesus, that it may come as something of a shock to know that it was a term already familiar to Jews when they spoke about God. 'Redeemer' is indeed a New Testament word, but one with a long Old Testament history. As with so much else in the New Testament, it is only against the backdrop provided by the Old that its later perspective can be adequately appreciated. Lacking this background, many Christians may even be surprised to be told that it is a 'picture' at all. They have heard it so often that they may have come to assume that it is simply a dogmatic proposition, a straightforward theological statement. Yet a picture of God it is in the Old Testament, a picture drawn straight from Israelite family life. To understand what it says about God, therefore, we need to know what the term meant in ancient Israelite society.

In ancient Israel there was a very strong sense of the relatedness of the family, and this applied not only to the narrower circle we today might describe as 'the nuclear family' but to what, again in modern sociological terminology, is often referred to as 'the extended family'. The law both recognised these strong ties of kinship and was designed to promote them. 'Honouring of parents' was one of the basic ten commandments and was seen as fundamental to the order of society (Exod. 20: 12, Deut. 5: 16). On the other hand, the wider extension of family loyalty is seen, for example, in the words of Abimelech addressed to the people of Shechem who are described as 'his mother's kinsmen . . . and the whole clan of his mother's family' (Ju. 9: 1.). Indeed, the same phrase can be used even by 'all the tribes of Israel' when speaking to David:

> Then all the tribes of Israel came to David at Hebron, and said, 'Behold, we are your bone and your flesh.' (II Sam. 5: 1)

With such a marked sense of relatedness, the law sought to give expression to the truth that, if any member of the family suffered, the loss was common to them all. If, for example, a kinsman became poor and had to sell land that had belonged to the family, it was a loss to them all, the whole family being thereby in a real sense 'weakened'. So the law includes prescriptions like the following:

> If your brother becomes poor and sells part of his property, then his next of kin shall come and redeem what his brother has sold. (Lev. 25: 25)

The verb translated by the RSV as 'to redeem' in the Hebrew is *gā'al* and the word rendered in the RSV and the NEB as 'next of kin' and in the JB by 'nearest relation' is a noun which is formed by the participle of that verb, *gô'ēl*. This is often translated, according to context, as 'next of kin' or 'nearest kinsman' or 'redeemer'. It describes some act of protecting of the poor by the nearest member of the family. Often this involves the act of 'buying back' and so of 'redeeming' that which was threatened with loss, for whatever reason. Naturally, it was realised that the nearest relation might not be able to afford to do this, whereupon the responsibility would pass to the next nearest relation. This becomes clear in Leviticus 25: 47 in the case of the poor relation who has had to sell himself into slavery:

> If a stranger or sojourner with you becomes rich, and your brother beside him becomes poor and sells himself to the stranger or sojourner with you, or to a member of the stranger's family, then after he is sold he may be redeemed; one of his brothers may redeem him, or a near kinsman belonging to his family may redeem him . . .

The Old Testament affords an interesting example of this law in relation to property. Jeremiah is approached by a cousin, Hanamel, who evidently has to sell his field, presumably to raise money. Hanamel says:

> 'Buy my field which is at Anathoth, for the right of redemption by purchase is yours . . . buy it for yourself.' (Jer. 32: 7)

Presumably Jeremiah was the next of kin to Hanamel and, by purchasing the land, would thus have kept the property within the ownership of the family. Just how important that was held to be is witnessed by Naboth's refusal to sell, even to the king, who was offering generous terms, land which was part of the family heritage.

> 'I will not give you the inheritance of my fathers.' (I Ki. 21: 4)

A strange extension of the law relating to nearest kinsman is shown by the practice of Levirate[1] marriage, found in Deuteronomy 25: 5-10. This is the only form in which we have this law and it probably dropped out of practice during the biblical period. Deuteronomy applies it only to the situation where the brothers were living together (presumably the only remaining case where it was likely to have been considered practical) and it realises that there can be no enforcement at law beyond the appeal to family obligation and perhaps the shaming of anyone who refused these obligations (vv. 9f.).

This law states that when a man dies, leaving a widow, but no son to inherit, rather than leave the widow to marry again outside the family the brother of the dead man shall perform the duty of husband to her, so that the first-born son to this union may take the dead man's name. Thus the 'name' of the dead man is perpetuated in his descendants (a very important concept in the Old Testament as long as there was no thought of a life after death). But there was more than 'honour' or memory at stake. The reference to the first 'son' and the stated design of the practice to avoid the need for the widow to marry outside the family (v. 5) shows that the main purpose was to keep the inheritance firmly within the dead man's family. (At that point only sons could inherit. By the time of the later law-code, the

'Priestly Code' already referred to, case law had established the precedent of the right of daughters to succeed. See Nu. 27: 1-11, especially v. 8).[2] A brother might refuse to act his part. It could be in his selfish interest to decline since, if he gave his sister-in-law a son, the property would pass to that son. If the widow remained childless, however, the land would be his. (This must be presumed to be so, although we do not in fact know very much about Israelite inheritance rights). In any event, if he did refuse, the widow's only redress was a public accusation and shaming of her brother-in-law with the symbolic act of pulling off his sandal (a sign of ownership of land, cf. Ruth 4: 7, cf. Amos 2: 6), spitting in his face and uttering a curse:

> 'So shall it be done to the man who does not build up his brother's house.' (Deut. 25: 9)

Thereafter the man's house would have gained the reputation of being, 'The house of him that had his sandal pulled off' (v. 10).

There are only two cases of Levirate marriage recorded in the Old Testament. The first is that of Tamar, recorded in Genesis chapter 38. Judah married his first son, Er, to Tamar, but when Er dies Judah addresses his second son, Onan, with that confident air of authority which appears to have characterised fatherhood in those days:

> 'Go in to your brother's wife, and perform the duty of a brother-in-law to her, and raise up offspring for your brother.' (v. 8)

But even in those days, apparently, parental authority, while it could command outward compliance, could not always control the feelings and motives of children. Onan does not complete the act of procreation, knowing that, if he does, there would be a risk of the inheritance passing to the son of the union (v. 9). For this, God strikes Onan dead. Judah, concerned at the mortality rate among his sons in liaison with Tamar (perhaps one of the earliest recorded instances of a *femme fatale*) witholds from her his third son, Shelah. By a strategem, however, she outwits him and secures a son for herself. Er's property remains safely with her line.

The other example of a Levirate marriage is that involving Ruth, the Moabitess, and Boaz, a kinsman of her Israelite mother-in-law, Naomi. The story of Ruth is of especial interest because it involves the responsibility of the *Gô'ēl* (i.e. 'next of kin', 'redeemer'), not only for Levirate marriage, but for the redemption of property. Naomi, her husband Elimelech, and their two sons, named unhappily but with sad prescience, Mahlon ('sickly') and Chilion ('wasting') emigrated to Moab at a time of famine in Judah. During their stay of ten years there, both Elimelech and the two sons died, leaving the widowed Naomi with her two widowed Moabitess daughters-in-law, Orpah and Ruth, whom the sons had married. On Naomi's return to Judah, Ruth insists on accompanying her in spite of Naomi's protesting that she has no more sons from whom to offer Ruth a husband. While gleaning in the fields of Boaz, Ruth attracts his attention. Boaz indeed would like to marry her, but there was a relation nearer than he who had the first right of claim to act as *Gô'ēl*. Boaz calls him to a public meeting of the elders of their town and mentions that Naomi has land to sell and that the kinsman has first right of redemption. The man is interested, but then Boaz lets it be known that this will also involve marrying Ruth and so acting as nearest kinsman to Naomi's dead husband, Elimelech, ensuring the rights of inheritance to his line. This, of course, would mean the danger of the land passing back to Elimelech's family and the man declines. Thereupon the way is open for Boaz both to redeem the land and marry Ruth in the happiest of endings. Interestingly, the bargain is sealed with the ceremonial withdrawal of a sandal (Ruth 4: 7ff.). There are a number of difficult legal details over which scholars disagree in their interpretation, largely, no doubt, because of our limited knowledge of such matters.[3]

After the use of the term *Gô'ēl* to describe the duty of a nearest kinsman to 'bale out' a poor relative and of the brother-in-law's responsibility in Levirate marriage, we should note another most significant aspect of the Hebrew understanding of the role of the *Gô'ēl*. That is the '*Gô'ēl* of Blood' or, as it is often rendered, 'The Avenger of Blood'. Again, it is concerned with the protection of the family. If a member of the family is murdered, then the blood that is spilled is understood as a loss to the order and well-being of the whole group. This loss can be restored only by blood vengeance against the guilty. The law of the 'Avenger of Blood' runs as follows:

> The murderer shall be put to death. The avenger of blood shall himself put the murderer to death: when he meets him he shall put him to death. (Nu. 35: 18b, 19, cf. 21b)

That occurs in the latest law-code in the Old Testament, the Priestly Code,[4] but the law itself is clearly much older as its appearance in Deuteronomy 19:12, and references to it in older parts of the Old Testament, suggest. In both Deuteronomy and the Priestly Code the law is clearly being regulated by the limitation of the term 'murderer' to the person who is guilty of deliberate killing, rather than what we should call 'manslaughter'. That is why 'cities of refuge' were established to protect the one guilty of manslaughter from the immediate anger of the next of kin. Such 'cities of refuge' are legislated for in Deuteronomy 19: 1-10 and Numbers 35: 22-28. Joshua 20: 1-9 purports to record the institution of such cities in the earliest days of the settlement. Whatever the date and circumstances of their origin, the passage no doubt offers valuable commentary on how they functioned in later Israelite life. Certainly the concept of 'sanctuary' which a refugee from justice could claim while he secured a proper hearing for his case is an ancient and widespread one. Centuries ago church buildings offered similar sanctuary to refugees from justice or vengeance.

Examples involving the rights and duties of the 'Avenger of Blood' in the Old Testament are to be found in Judges 8: 18-21 where Gideon avenges the blood of his brothers at the hands of the Midianites. He does so, it is recorded, uttering the words,

> 'They were my brothers, the sons of my mother.' (v. 19)

Again, the Gibeonites induced David to avenge Saul's sons for their father's massacre of some of their tribe (II Sam. 21: 1-6), although this may have been regarded as an exceptional case involving non-Israelites. Probably it was the (fictitious) story which the wise woman of Tekoa related to David which enshrined the more customary form of the practice. She claimed to have had two sons, one of whom killed the other following a fierce argument. She appeals to the king:

> 'And now the whole family has risen against your handmaid, and they say, "Give up the man who struck his brother that we may kill him for the life of the brother whom he slew."' (II Sam. 14: 7)

The aim of the wise woman by this contrived story is to secure Absalom's return and she tells it at Joab's instigation. If it had not been a typical case, however, the king is unlikely to have been convinced by it. Here again we note the concern of the immediate family for blood revenge but, in this case, the widow is seeking to invoke the power and authority of the king to protect the right of succession and inheritance in her own family (v. 7).

We are now in a position to see the full force of the words of God recorded in Genesis 4: 10 following the murder of Abel by his brother Cain. God says to Cain:

> 'The voice of your brother's blood is crying to me from the ground.'

It calls out for the protection and vengeance of the *Gô'ēl*. But in this instance the nearest kinsman is the murderer, and by the fiction of the story there is no other. So God himself assumes the role of *Gô'ēl*. However, it is noteworthy that he does not retaliate by killing Cain. On the contrary, he 'marks' him by an act of special protective, divine grace (v. 15). God as the *Gô'ēl* is concerned for the protection of humankind, all of whom are his kindred. Protection of the line in this case demands grace and forgiveness, not the retaliation of blood vengeance. Such a truth is probably hinted at by the wise woman of Tekoa as she gets nearer to the point of the story. David should act mercifully to his rebel son, Absalom, and recall him from exile. The text is obscure, but NEB renders, 'We shall all die: we shall be like water that is spilled on the ground and lost: but God will spare the man who does not set himself to keep the outlaw in banishment' (II Sam. 14: 14). David should show mercy and so limit the consequences of blood vengeance. It is clear that there are times when true protection of the family demands mercy and not the full rigour of punishment.

This brings us to something basic about the Old Testament use of the picture of *Gô'ēl*, Redeemer, to describe God. Underlying it is the conviction of the kinship between God and his people. God is not a disinterested, detached observer of their fortunes and misfortunes. He himself is bound up with their welfare. His concern is to protect his family, the people of Israel. This underlying note of kinship is made explicit in Isaiah 63:8f.:

> For he said, 'Surely they are my people,
> sons who will not deal falsely';
> and he became their Saviour.
> In all their affliction he was afflicted . . .
> in his love and pity he redeemed them;
> he lifted them up and carried them . . .

It is, perhaps, no accident that by far the greatest number of references to God as *Gô'ēl* speak of his deliverance at the time of the Exodus from Egypt. There he acted as kinsman to protect them from the exploitation and oppression of those outside the family. So the 'Song of the Sea' reads:

> Thou hast led in thy steadfast love
> the people whom thou hast redeemed,
> thou hast guided them by thy strength
> to thy holy abode. (Exod. 15: 13)

This was the fulfilment of the promise God had made to Moses when he appeared to him and called him to the task of leading the Israelites out of Egypt:

> 'Say therefore to the people of Israel, "I am the LORD, and I will bring you out from under the burden of the Egyptian, and I will deliver you from their bondage, and I will redeem you with an outstretched arm and with great acts of judgement."' (Exod. 6: 6)

Indeed, it might be said that, by the slaughter of all the first-born of Egypt, God acted as 'blood-avenger' for his oppressed people. Certainly, the 'Song of Moses' says:

> Praise his people, O you nations;
> for he avenges the blood of his servants . . . (Deut. 32: 43)

However, this is not made explicit in references to the Exodus, where the stress is usually laid on the divine intention to deliver his people from the servitude of slavery, just as a *Gô'ēl*'s task, if he could afford it, was to redeem one of the family who had been sold into slavery.

> So he saved them from the hand of the foe,
> And redeemed them from the power of the enemy. (Ps. 106: 10)

In view of the centrality of the Exodus as the supreme example of God's power and will to act as *Gô'ēl* for his people, it is not surprising to find it prominent in the work of Second Isaiah.[5] He predicts the return from the slavery of exile in Babylon as a second Exodus from Egypt. However, it will be so miraculous that it will transcend the first Exodus as a demonstration of God's power and will to save.

> Thus says the LORD,
> who makes a way in the sea,
> a path in the mighty waters,
> who brings forth chariot and horse,
> army and warrior . . .
> 'Remember not the former things,
> nor consider the things of old.
> Behold, I am doing a new thing . . .
> I will make a way in the wilderness
> and rivers in the desert.' (Isa. 43: 16ff.)

Here the 'former things' refers to the tradition of the Exodus from Egypt, the foundation doctrine of Israel's faith and the ground of their life as God's people. The 'new thing' will so eclipse that in splendour, power and grace that they need no longer mention it, important as it was. Unlike that first escape which was 'in haste' (cf. Exod. 12: 11, Deut. 16: 3), this will be a peaceful and orderly exit, unthreatened by any foe:

> For you shall not go out in haste,
> and you shall not go in flight,
> for the LORD will go before you,
> and the God of Israel will be your rearguard. (Isa. 52: 12)

The last two lines refer to the guidance of God in the desert after the Exodus when he went before them as a pillar of fire by night and of cloud by day (Exod. 13: 21). When they were threatened from behind, however, tradition had it that the pillar 'moved from before them and stood behind them' (Exod. 14: 19). But now, with the return from Babylon, the cry will go up:

> Sing, O heavens, for the LORD has done it;
> shout, O depths of the earth . . .
> For the LORD has *redeemed* Jacob,
> and will be glorified in Israel.

Or again,

> Break forth together into singing,
> you waste places of Jerusalem;
> for the LORD has comforted his people,
> he has *redeemed* Jerusalem. (Isa. 52: 9)

Now, therefore, Israel need fear no foe:

> But now thus says the LORD,
> he who created you, O Jacob . . .
> 'Fear not, for I have *redeemed* you.' (Isa. 43: 1)

Moreover, they can return to Yahweh from their sin and failure and trust in his mercy:

> I have swept away your transgressions like a cloud,
> and your sins like mist;
> return to me, for I have *redeemed* you. (Isa. 44: 22)

The title 'Redeemer of Israel' or its equivalent, in fact, appears so many times in Second Isaiah, that it must be counted as one of the principle themes of his prophecy. It is no wonder, that with such an understanding of God's relation to them, the concept of

God as Redeemer should often have become the basis of prayer to Yahweh to act as kinsman to the community as a whole.

> Remember thy congregation,
> which thou hast gotten of old,
> which thou hast redeemed to be the tribe of thy heritage! (Ps. 74: 2)

That Psalm was written in the circumstance of invasion by powerful enemies. Second Isaiah's words came as answer to such laments. So do words found in Jeremiah 50: 34, spoken to the people and their leaders in exile:

> Their Redeemer is strong; the LORD of hosts is his name. He will surely plead their cause, that he may give rest to the earth . . . .'

It is natural that a concept which was so bound up with the protection and care of the individual member of the family should give rise to the idea of God as *Gô'ēl*, not only of the nation, but of each individual Israelite. In a real sense, each individual is 'kinsman' to Yahweh. He can, therefore, look with expectation to him to act as 'nearest kinsman' when all others have failed. So the writer of Lamentations can say:

> Thou hast taken up my cause, O Lord,
> thou hast redeemed my life.' (Lam. 3: 58)[6]

Or again, the individual can pray:

> Draw near to me, redeem me,
> set me free because of my enemies! (Ps. 69: 18)

Just as with the picture of God as Judge, the zealous concern of God for the oppressed individual could be turned against the powerful exploiters in the nation.

> Do not remove an ancient landmark
> or enter the fields of the fatherless;
> for their Redeemer is strong;
> he will plead their cause against you. (Prov. 23: 10f.)

Yahweh, as *Gô'ēl*, is a powerful advocate on his people's behalf in court, able to secure justice against their influential adversaries. God as Redeemer and God as Judge turn out to be very closely related pictures.

One of the most interesting cases of the individual seeking a *Gô'ēl's* help is that of Job. This righteous man, who feels he has been unjustly judged by his losses and his suffering, wrestles, not only with his own pain and anger, but with the mystery of God's righteousness. He wonders how his 'cause' can ever be pleaded before this God.

> O earth, cover not my blood,
> and let my cry find no resting place. (Jb. 16: 18)

This cry evokes the words of God to Cain about Abel, already cited, 'The voice of your brother's blood is crying to me from the ground.' (Gen. 4: 10). Job pleads that his cry will come to the attention of a *Gô'ēl* and secure his intervention on Job's behalf. In a moment of faith he cries out:

> But in my heart I know that my vindicator (*Gô'ēl*) lives
> and that he will rise at last to speak in court;
> and I shall discern my witness standing at my side
> and see my defending counsel, even God himself,
> whom I shall see with my own eyes,
> I myself, and no other.' (Jb. 19: 23-27, NEB)

There are many obscurities in the text here which prevent certain translation. Norman Snaith, wrote that it could only be taken as a promise of life after death '. . . by a most liberal latitude in translation, a strong attachment to the Latin version, and reminiscences of Handel's Messiah'![7] What does appear here, is that, as in chapter 16, Job comes to see that his advocate with God, his *Gô'ēl*, can be no other than God himself. God will take up his case as his *Gô'ēl* and he will be vindicated. This is not yet a hope of an after-life, as Snaith rightly argued, but it is a conviction that in this life he will be championed in his weakness and suffering by God who will take his part.

It is little wonder that this should become the basis for an ultimate hope for an oppressed and beleaguered nation. So a prophet, picturing the final Paradisical state of Israel after God's deliverance can say,

> No lion shall be there,
> nor shall any ravenous beast come up on it;
> they shall not be found there,
> but the redeemed shall walk there.
> And the ransomed of the LORD shall return,
> and come to Zion with singing;
> everlasting joy shall be upon their heads;
> they shall obtain joy and gladness,
> and sorrow and sighing shall flee away. (Isa. 35: 9f.)

Just as it could be said of the ideal king in Jerusalem,

> He has pity on the weak and the needy, and saves the lives of the needy. From oppression and violence he *redeems* their life; and precious is their blood in his sight. (Ps. 72: 13f.)

so, at the last, it will be when Yahweh reigns as true king:

> Break forth together into singing,
> you waste places of Jerusalem;
> for the LORD has comforted his people,
> he has *redeemed* Jerusalem.
> The LORD has bared his holy arm
> before the eyes of all nations;
> and all the ends of the earth shall see
> the salvation of our God. (Isa. 52: 9f.)

The God who by his grace is kinsman to his people Israel and to every weak and needy individual within its community; the one who 'protects' them by taking vengeance on their oppressors because he has power to act as their redeemer; the one, therefore, to whom individual and nation can cry in prayer confident that he will hear; the one, however, who knows when mercy and forgiveness may break the chain of blood vengeance and be a more sure protection and guarantee of the life and salvation of his people—this is the God who can be characterised in the Old Testament as 'Redeemer'.

NOTES TO CHAPTER ONE

1. The term 'Levirate' comes from the Latin word 'Levir' meaning 'a husband's brother'.

2. See Introduction above, n. 8.

3. An interesting recent study of the legal aspects of the Book of Ruth is that by Anthony Phillips, 'The Book of Ruth—Deception and Shame', *Journal of Jewish Studies*, 37, 1986, pp. 1-17.

4. See Introduction, n. 8.

5. See Introduction, n. 14.

6. It is, of course, always possible that the speaker in any given case is seen as the personification of the whole community, be he king, prophet or, perhaps, in this case, the whole community of Jerusalem. But the use of such a literary form shows how it was understood that the individual could, and often did, take this way of thinking to himself for his own use.

7. N.H. Snaith, *The Distinctive Ideas of the Old Testament*, London, 1944, p.90n.

II

GOD AS CRAFTSMAN

There is something of the creator in all of us. Especially for those who sit at desks all day or are confined to repetitive and monotonous work, to create something, whether it be a cake, a set of kitchen cabinets, a painting, a carving—or even a book—can be a rich, not to say therapeutic activity. Seeing something tangible for our effort can be a satisfying way of expressing ourselves, however unskilfully we do it.

Perhaps it is this deep longing to create and enjoy the creation of others which makes art galleries, theatres and concert halls still magnets to so many. Indeed, the health of a society can be measured by its arts and the priority it gives to the arts. Perhaps the fingerprints of our values are seen in the products of our artists and craftsmen.

That is why one of the most evocative and powerful means of understanding the life of an ancient civilisation, including Israel, is that afforded by its pottery and other artefacts, often the only kind of its artistic creations to survive. For archaeologists, pottery remains offer help not only in reconstructing the life of the people, but in dating levels of excavation and so providing a chronological 'grid' by which the history of a society can be plotted. But, beyond that, the best of the artefacts reflect a very great technical skill and artistic imagination. They both served the basic needs of a community and gave a decorative and artistic richness to its life. It is not difficult, therefore, to understand why the potter, or, indeed, the wood carver and metal smith, were held in such high esteem.

The Old Testament reflects this sense of wonder at the skill of such workers. Jer. 10: 9, for example, acknowledges the skill and workmanship of craftsmen even if it is felt that their products too often are put to foolish uses by those who practise idolatry:

> Beaten silver is brought from Tarshish,
> and gold from Uphaz.
> They are the work of the craftsman
> and of the hands of the goldsmith;
> their clothing is violet and purple;
> they are all the work of skilled men. (Jer. 10: 9)

Indeed, Bezalel, the master craftsman in charge of the décor of the temple, had such skills that they could be attributable only to the inspiration of God's spirit:

> See, I have called by name Bezalel . . . and I have filled him with the spirit of God, with ability and intelligence, with knowledge and all craftsmanship, to devise artistic designs, to work in gold, silver and bronze, and cutting stones for setting, and in carving wood for work in every craft. (Exod. 31: 2-5).

It is hardly surprising that human artistic ability should be attributed to the inspiration of God's spirit when, as we shall see in this chapter, God himself can be pictured as a great, master craftsman.

This admiration for skill in what might be called the 'plastic' arts like woodcarving, metalwork and pottery, could be extended to the design and construction of fine buildings. The temple which Solomon built and for which he employed celebrated craftsmen such as Hiram (I Ki. 7: 13f.) could be described as an 'exalted house' (I Ki. 8: 13), a term which depicts not only its elevation but its noble appearance. In the same way Ezekiel, apostrophising the city of Tyre, can say 'your builders made perfect your beauty (Ezek. 27: 4)'. There follows an elaborate and skilful metaphor in which Tyre is said to be like a beautiful ship on which skilled craftsmen spent their labour.

There are many facets to the skill and artistry of the craftsman. He or she must be more than a mere technician who has the facility of hand to execute the designs and thoughts of

GOD AS CRAFTSMAN

others. There has to be also the imagination and flair to *conceive* the work before anything has been done towards its creation. This is reflected in a most interesting way in the Old Testament. The Hebrew word which is used most often of such work as pottery is the verb 'to form' or 'to fashion' (Heb. *yāṣar*). Yet the same verb has another range of meaning altogether. It also means 'to devise' and so 'to conceive' an idea or a project.

Another facet of the craftsman's work is the skill in actually bringing the 'design' or 'conception' to life. Many of us may have seen a 'picture' in our mind's eye which we long to reproduce, but we lack the technical skill to do anything like justice to it when we splodge resistant oils onto stubborn canvas. And the sorry mess most of us make, both of ourselves and our materials if we try beginners' evening classes in pottery, is a far cry from what we had imagined ourselves shaping on the wheel. We shall see how both these aspects of God as craftsman are the theme of wonder and praise in the Old Testament—his wonderful designs and purposes on the one hand, and his power and skill in bringing them to fruition on the other. Obviously all this is part of the celebration of God as Creator, both of the universe as a whole and of individual men and women. But it passes easily from this to celebration of God as Lord of History who is working throughout time to bring his purposes of love and grace to fulfilment.

Again, we may assume that a craftsman or architect has a special feeling towards a work he or she has created in so far as it expresses what was in the mind of its creator. Such feelings must include pride in achievement, a sense of fulfilment and, surely, of love and concern for the work created. If the work stubbornly refuses to express what was in the mind and imagination, then the frustration, perhaps even the anger, must be commensurately strong.

Finally, we must note, however, that this is a very one-sided picture when applied to God. It stresses entirely the initiative and power of the craftsman and the complete passivity of that which is created, which plays no part in its own inception. It owes everything to its maker. This aspect also appears in the Old Testament, but perhaps it warns us of the limitations of each picture among the many offered to us in illustrating the relationship between God and his creation. Each needs to be supplemented by other pictures, in this case, for instance, by that of God's being also like a parent with children. For while children play no part in their procreation, they do develop minds of their own from the very earliest stages, as every parent can testify. The subsequent relationship of parents and children is increasingly a two-way one.

We do not have to go far into the Old Testament before we come across the picture of God as craftsman. After the first account of creation in Genesis 1:1- 2: 4a we find a second in 2: 4b-25, in some ways a simpler, even more 'folksy' picture in which God is one of the actors on the stage of the world he has created. It is highly sophisticated theologically, however, and we should not let its 'anthropomorphism' (speaking of God in human terms) lead us to condescend towards it or patronise it. It is often said to belong to the 'Yahwistic' Source of the Pentateuch, so-called because it maintains that people worshipped God by the name 'Yahweh' from earliest times (Gen. 4: 26).[1] Now, in this story we read:

> Then the LORD God *formed* man ['ādām or humankind] of dust from the ground . . . (Gen. 2: 7)

The Hebrew verb 'formed' is *yāṣar*, the verb that is used most frequently of the activity of the potter. Like a potter, God works from clay, forming the human being in his hands. Indeed, there is a play on words in the idea of humanity coming from the clay of the ground, for the Hebrew word for the human being is *'ādām*, and the word for ground is *'ᵃdāmâh*. The two are related, and it was by the power and skill of the divine Craftsman that the one was formed from the other. Indeed, his is a 'Pygmalion-type' piece of craftsmanship for

> he breathed into his nostrils the breath of life; and man became a living being. (v. 7).

That is something human artists have been able to do only in legend. Indeed, many scholars believe that, behind this way in which the Yahwist expresses his idea of the creation of humankind, lie older Ancient Near Eastern myths. In an Akkadian epic of the creation of man by the Mother Goddess, we read of Nintu, the goddess, saying to the other deities, 'Let him (i.e. 'man') be formed out of clay, be animated with blood.' In fact the clay is animated by the blood of a slain god, whereas, in the Yahwist's account, it is the 'breath' of God which brings him to life. Both, however, bear testimony to the awareness that human beings are ambivalent creatures compounded of the 'earthy', yet with elements of the 'divine' in their make-up. This thought excited the praise of the Psalmist as he contemplated the wonder of God's 'craftsmanship':

> When I look at thy heavens, *the work of thy fingers*,
> the moon and the stars which thou hast established;
> what is man that thou art mindful of him?
> and the son of man that thou dost care for him?
> Yet thou hast made him little less than God,
> and dost crown him with glory and honour.
> Thou hast given him dominion over *the works of thy hands;*
> thou hast put all things under his feet . . . (Ps. 8: 3-6)

Genesis 2: 19 tells us that God, the craftsman, had *formed* every creature:

> So out of the ground the LORD God *formed* every beast of the field and every bird of the air . . .

but he had put them under the control of the supreme act of his craftsmanship, the human being:

> . . .and he brought them to the man to see what he would call them . . .

'Naming' is a sign of control in the Old Testament, as when, for example, the Egyptians showed their control over their puppet king Eliakim by renaming him Jehoiakim (II Ki. 23: 34).

Another Psalmist contemplates the mystery and miracle of his own creation from the time when he was 'unformed' (the Aramaic equivalent of the Hebrew word 'unformed' used in v. 16 means 'an unfinished vessel'):

> For thou didst form [a different Hebrew verb] my
>   inward parts,
> thou didst knit me together in my mother's womb.
> I praise thee, for thou art fearful and wonderful.
> Wonderful are thy works!
> Thou knowest me right well;
> my frame was not hidden from thee,
> when I was being made in secret,
> intricately wrought in the depths of the earth.
> Thy eyes beheld my *unformed* substance;
> in thy book were written every one of them,
> the days that were formed for me,
> when as yet there was none of them. (Ps. 139: 13-16)

Not only is this a theme of wonder and praise in itself, but it leads on to the idea of God's power and care for his workmanship.

> He who formed the eye, does he not see . . . ? (Ps. 94: 9)

And this leads to the climax of the argument:

> the LORD knows the thoughts of a person . . . (v. 11).

Similarly, Psalm 33 argues *from* the power of God as a creating craftsman *to* his knowledge:

> The LORD looks down from heaven,
> he sees all the sons of men . . .
> he who *fashions* the hearts of them all,
> and observes all their deeds. (v. 13)

The Servant of the LORD, who knows opposition and frustration in his ministry, yet draws comfort from the power of the God who 'made' him to care for him and make his mission prosper:

> And now the LORD says,
> who *formed* me from the womb to be his servant . . .
> I am honoured in the eyes of the LORD,
> and my God has become my strength . . . . (Isa. 49: 5)

It is indeed the thought of the *power* of God the craftsman that is often to the fore:

> Thus says the LORD, who stretched out the heavens and founded the earth and formed the spirit of man within him: 'Lo, I am about to make Jerusalem a cup of reeling to all the peoples round about it . . . .' (Zech. 12: 1)

The passage goes on to give assurance of God's intention to deliver Jerusalem from the attacks of her enemies.

Of course, the picture also evokes thoughts of God's tender compassion towards his handiwork:

> For he knows our frame [the Hebrew noun derives from the verb *yāṣar*]
> he remembers that we are dust. (Ps. 103: 14)

In other words he remembers the human being's creaturely dependence and weakness and acts accordingly, as tenderly and carefully as any craftsman to a work of his own creation in which he takes pleasure. Indeed, his pleasure as craftsman is one real reason for his action in creating at all. So he will bring all his people back from exile,

> Because you are precious in my eyes,
> and honoured, and I love you . . .
> Fear not, for I am with you;
> I will bring your offspring from the east,
> and from the west I will gather you . . .
> (I will) bring my sons from afar
> and my daughters from the ends of the earth,
> everyone who is called by my name,
> whom I *created* for my glory,
> whom I *formed and made*. (Isa. 43: 4-7)

Naturally, God's power and artistic inspiration are revealed in the creation of the universe in all its grandeur, regularity and beauty:

> For thus says the LORD,
> who created the heavens . . .
> who formed the earth and made it . . .

> he did not create it a chaos,
> he formed it to be inhabited. (Isa. 45: 18)

This absence of 'chaos' from God's creation is seen in the orderly cycle of the seasons:

> Thou hast fixed all the bounds of the earth;
> thou hast made summer and winter. (Ps. 74: 17)

He it is who keeps the powerful forces of the seas in check:

> The sea is his, for he made it;
> for his hands formed the dry land. (Ps. 95: 5)

In the same way he is responsible for the ordering of day and night:

> I form light and create darkness . . . (Isa. 45: 7)

Nevertheless, the thought keeps returning to that of the power of this great craftsman-creator exercised in his care and love for his people:

> Not like these [the worthless idols] is he
> who is the portion of Jacob,
> for he is the one who formed all things,
> and Israel is the tribe of his inheritance;
> the LORD of hosts is his name. (Jer. 51: 19)

Indeed, like the master craftsman, God has a purpose which he has all along conceived and he has the skill and power to bring it to fruition in his creation:

> 'I have spoken, and I will bring it to pass;
> I have *purposed* (Heb. *yāṣar*),
> and I will do it.' (Isa. 46: 11)

Here we encounter that double meaning of the Hebrew verb *yāṣar* already noted. The same verb which does duty for the actual 'forming' or 'creating' of something, also means 'to devise', 'to plan' or 'to purpose'. This means among other things, that

GOD AS CRAFTSMAN

even if powerful enemies oppress God's people, far from deflecting the design of the master-craftsman, they are often serving it. So, of the Assyrian who is arrogantly proud of his power and achievements in his campaign against Judah and Jerusalem, the prophet can say in God's name:

> Have you not heard
> that I determined it long ago?
> I planned (Heb. *yāṣar*) from days of old
> what now I bring to pass . . . . (II Ki. 19: 25, cf. Isa. 37: 26)

For there can be no doubt, as these words imply, that to achieve his long-term purpose for his people, God may well 'purpose' their judgement or punishment. No doubt the process of being created, of roughness being smoothed down and imperfections eradicated, could be a long and painful process if an artefact were conscious. The *people* God is creating *are* conscious and do often express the painfulness of the process. No one puts it more clearly than Jeremiah with his act of prophetic symbolism in visiting a potter at work. He sees the vessel that is being shaped go wrong. It did not sufficiently resemble that which the craftsman had in mind for it. So the potter reduced the vessel to its original lumpen mass and began again:

> Then the word of the LORD came to me: 'O house of Israel, can I not do with you as this potter has done? says the LORD. Behold, like the clay in the potter's hand, so are you in my hand, O house of Israel.' (Jer. 18: 5f.)

It is just for this reason that, in a remarkable play on words, God says to the people of Israel:

> Behold, I am *shaping* (Heb. *yāṣar*) evil against you. (Jer. 18: 11)

They are to be taken back to their first state (like slaves in Egypt) in the exile to Babylon, so that God can rework them into what he really designed them to be.

An even more severe picture of God as potter judging his people is to be found in the next chapter. There Jeremiah is commanded to go and purchase an earthen jar (19: 1f.) which he is solemnly to break in the presence of some of the leading members of the Judean 'establishment' (v. 10). Far from being moist clay which the potter could rework (as in ch. 18) this is a finished jar which, once broken, is irreparable.

> 'So I will break this people and this city, as one breaks a potter's vessel, so that it can never be mended.' (Jer.19: 11)

That seems to match poorly with the picture in the previous chapter, of God remaking what has been spoiled on the potter's wheel. Probably, behind the earlier picture in chapter 18 is an original word of Jeremiah who saw some hope in the future for the community (even although the chapter has been reworked by Deuteronomistic editors).[2] In chapter 19, however, we hear those Deuteronomists speaking in the exile, explaining why the state of Judah and the city of Jerusalem do seem to have been broken beyond repair. Perhaps the fact that Jeremiah is pictured there as having taken some of the priests and elders of the community (v. 1) and that it is 'this people and this city' which are to be shattered in the coming judgement (v. 19, cf. vv. 11-13) suggest that, in the view of the editors, it is the organised state with its religious institutions which was to be shattered. This would never be remodelled in quite the same way as it existed before the exile as an independent monarchy. God's purpose for his people would be pursued apart from the structures which had become so hopelessly corrupt. The devastating effect of the destruction of the city can be commented on with bitter irony in the exilic Lamentations:

> The precious sons of Zion,
> worth their weight in fine gold,
> how are they reckoned as earthen pots,
> the work of a potter's hands! (Lam. 4: 2)

In irony, the very opposite deduction is drawn from the pride Yahweh feels in the work of his hands. They are no longer as valuable or as durable as gold. They have shown all the fragility and weakness of cheap pottery. They have been 'shattered' in God's hands.

This is the picture which, as we have said, stresses the passivity of human beings. Like the picture of the shepherd and the sheep it can be distortedly one-sided if taken alone. The sometimes stupid docility of the sheep does not say all there is to be said about human responsibility before God, any more than that of the inanimate submission of clay in the hands of the potter. Yet much in the Old Testament suggests that before the wisdom, power and infinite majesty of God, the only proper human response is faith, *one* element of which is submission to the divine purpose. The calmness of such faith which accepts the ways of God and bows to them is well pictured by a prophet following the return from exile. He sees the tragic aftermath of destruction and exile. Social, moral and religious chaos appear on all sides.

> Behold, thou wast angry, and we sinned;
> in our sins we have been a long time,
> and shall we be saved? . . .
> There is none that calls upon thy name,
> that bestirs himself to take hold of thee;
> for thou hast hid thy face from us,
> and hast delivered us into the hand of our iniquities . . . .
> Thy holy cities have become a wilderness,
> Zion has become a wilderness,
> Jerusalem a desolation. (Isa. 64: 5b, 7, 10).

In anguish and impatience it is natural that they should cry out:

> O that thou wouldst rend the heavens and come down,
> that the mountains might quake at thy presence . . .
> to make thy name known to thy adversaries,
> and that the nations might tremble at thy presence!' (vv. 1f.)

They are longing for another revelation of God in his power like that at Mount Sinai when God first came to them at the beginning of their national life as a covenant people. Yet, in all their longing to see the great events of their history repeated, the prophet can utter a prayer of quiet trust, appealing to the picture of the craftsman God:

> Yet, O LORD, thou art our father;
> we are the clay, and thou art our potter;
> we are all the work of thy hand.

Second Isaiah also remonstrates with the people for failing to show this spirit of quiet acceptance of God's wisdom and power. When he brings the news that God is about to answer their cries, in fact to 'rend the heavens' and come quickly down to deliver them, he announces that it will be through the instrumentality of the Persian ruler, Cyrus. God has raised up Cyrus and ordained his march of military victory in order that he might be the means of his people's release from their captivity in Babylon.

> He [i.e. God] says of Cyrus, 'He is my shepherd,
> and he shall fulfil all my purpose';
> saying of Jerusalem, 'She shall be built',
> and of the temple, 'Your foundations shall be laid.' (Isa. 44: 28).

Indeed, the prophet goes so far as to say that Cyrus is God's 'anointed'. The Hebrew word for 'anointed' is 'Messiah', elsewhere used only of the Davidic king. Clearly, for some loyal and pious Jews, this was going too far. How could the God of Israel use a pagan general for his purpose? The prophet has little patience with such myopic orthodoxy, and rebukes them with the picture of God as skilful craftsman:

> Woe to him who strives with his Maker,
> an earthen vessel with the potter!
> Does the clay say to him who fashions it,
> 'What are you making?'
> or, 'Your work has no handles?' . . .
> Thus says the LORD,
> the Holy One of Israel, and his Maker . . .
> 'Will you question me about my children,
> or command me concerning the work of my hands?'
> I made the earth,
> and created man upon it;
> it was my hands that stretched out the heavens,
> and I commanded all their host.
> I have aroused him (i.e. Cyrus) in righteousness,
> and I will make straight all his ways;

> he shall build my city
> and set my exiles free . . . (Isa. 45: 9, 11-13)

The picture of God as craftsman, then, perhaps says more of God than it does of man, yet it has its message for people. It speaks of God's great purposes of beauty, order and love which he has the power to bring to expression. This power is seen in the created universe, but even more in the supreme work of his craftsmanship, men and women themselves in all the mystery and wonder of their creation. They may rest confident in the care and strength of the one who has so created them for, like any craftsman, God takes pride and joy in his workmanship. Indeed, he has created them for his glory and to fulfil his purposes. If the material with which he works proves stubborn and intractable, God will not hesitate to undo and remake what is spoiled, but only in order that it may ultimately achieve his design. The person, the state, the nation, even the religious community which fails to respond to that purpose will know the pain of destruction and re-moulding. To such power, wisdom and love human beings should submit themselves in quiet trust and obedience. In the end, through all frustration, it is the purpose of God, as maker and craftsman, to 'build up', to create and to perfect. Out of all that is marred he intends, ultimately, to recreate.

> For, behold, I create new heavens
> and a new earth;
> and the old things shall not be remembered
> or come to mind. (Isa. 65: 17)

> For as the new heavens and the new earth
> which I will make
> shall remain before me, says the LORD;
> so shall your descendants remain.
> From new moon to new moon,
> and from sabbath to sabbath,
> all flesh shall come to worship before me,
> says the LORD. (Isa. 66: 22f.)

The last word is with God who, as Artist and Craftsman, creates and recreates to perfect all the purposes he has in mind for his creation.

NOTES TO CHAPTER TWO

1. This is the name given to the editor/writer of perhaps the earliest layer of the Pentateuch (the first five books of the Bible). It is so called because this source believes that the name 'Yahweh' for God had been known from the earliest times (Gen. 4: 26. Note that whenever the English Versions give the name 'LORD' in capital letters, it stands for the Hebrew name 'Yahweh'). Other sources believe that the name 'Yahweh' was revealed later in the time of Moses (see Exod. 3: 15 and 6: 3).

2. We shall come across several references to the 'Deuteronomists' in the course of these studies. Most scholars date the final form of the Book of Deuteronomy to the 7th. century BCE (although it contains older material and also shows signs of later editing during the time of the Babylonian exile in the 6th. century). Two other parts of the Old Testament in particular show the powerful influence of Deuteronomy in vocabulary, style and theology. These are the 'history' books, Joshua, Judges, Samuel and Kings and also the Book of Jeremiah. The name often given to the history books is 'The Deuteronomistic History' since it appears that, while they contain many early sources and traditions, they have been finally edited by people like those who produced the Book of Deuteronomy. The aim of these editors was to give a theological explanation for the disaster of the exile and to call the people to repentance. The Book of Jeremiah is also thought to have passed through their hands. The present form of this book represents their 'exposition' of the teaching of Jeremiah to the Jewish exiles in Babylon. This book, as they edited it, also calls for the repentance of the exiles, and assures them of God's intention to deliver them in the future if they do so repent.

III

GOD AS FATHER

Sometimes pictures which have been hanging on display for a long time become darkened and discoloured with the passage of the years. They need some cleaning and restoring to blaze out again with the vividness and force they must have had for those who first saw them. It is just so with the Old Testament 'pictures' of God. Some still communicate immediately and powerfully to us, like the picture of God as 'Craftsman'. The human experiences of creating and the appreciation of skill and beauty do not change fundamentally, even if superficial changes of taste occur from generation to generation and culture to culture. However, we have already seen that a picture like that of 'God as Redeemer' did need some work done on it before it could really be intelligible to us.

At first glance it might seem that the idea of God as 'Father' would be one which needs no touching up. It is a relationship built into human life for all time. Yet such an impression can be mistaken. We do not need to travel far to realise that very different concepts of the status, authority and position of the 'father' in the family obtain, even among different cultures today. For example, with large Asian communities in many western countries it is easy to observe cultures which are much more 'patriarchal' than those which have become customary in western, urban society. Often, Asian wives appear to defer to their husbands in a way that few western husbands have come to expect and which few of them receive. Asian fathers appear to exercise a control and discipline over their young which western fathers scarcely now attempt. If such gaps exist between ethnic groups in one society, what differences may not exist between our own customs and those of a near eastern culture separated from us by many centuries?

The bulk of our evidence for what 'fatherhood' meant in ancient Israel has to come from the Old Testament itself. Israel would almost certainly have to be described as a 'patriarchal' society, although we should not miss the high place given to women and the influence they could wield within it, a matter to be discussed in the last chapter (and indeed we must add that closer familiarity with Asian cultural groups today may give us similar surprises). Israelite families are usually described as the *beth 'ab*, that is, 'the father's house'. Genealogies are usually given through the father's line. The nearest relative is counted as being on the father's side of the family (e.g. Lev. 25: 9, where the Hebrew word for 'uncle', *dôd*, is used specifically of the father's brother). Speaking of the Hebrew family, R. de Vaux has said:

> In the normal type of Israelite marriage the husband is the 'master', the *ba'al*, (the Hebrew word means 'husband' or 'lord') of his wife. The father had absolute authority over his children, even over his married sons if they lived with him, and over their wives. In early times this authority included even the power over life and death: thus Judah condemned to death his daughter-in-law Tamar when she was accused of misconduct (Gen. 38: 24).[1]

We have also to be aware that the word 'father' can be used in an extended sense as well as to describe the (to us) more familiar, immediate relationship of father and son. It is certainly often used in the latter, more immediate sense, as when Solomon is recorded as praying:

> 'Now, therefore, O LORD, God of Israel, keep with thy servant David my father what thou hast promised him . . .' (I Ki. 8: 23)

Here the sense is obvious and literal. Yet Abraham is promised that he will be 'the father of a multitude of nations' (Gen. 17: 4) and this is obviously an extended fatherhood, meaning 'ancestor' to many future generations. This is the sense in which it is used by Second Isaiah when he addresses the despondent exiles with words from God:

> Look to Abraham your father
> and to Sarah who bore you;
> for when he was but one I called him,
> and I blessed him and made him many. (Isa. 51: 2)

John the Baptist is recorded by Matthew as rebuking the Judeans of his time with the words, '. . . do not presume to say to yourselves, "We have Abraham as our father" . . .' (Mt. 3:9). In a slightly more restricted sense Jacob's family is seen to extend to three generations (Gen. 46: 8-26) and the 'family' would be thought to include servants, resident aliens, widows and orphans who would depend on the head of the family for protection. An even wider sense is found in Genesis 4: 20 where it is said, 'Jabal was the father of all who dwell in tents and have cattle'; that is, he was the first of the line of nomads. This broader use of 'family' relationship is also seen in the Hebrew idiom to denote a group. Thus 'prophets' as a group can be described as 'sons of prophets'. Human beings can be described in general as 'son(s) of man'.

Certainly the 'father', who was seen as the head of family, held an honoured place, together with his wife. The Decalogue calls on Israelites to '*honour* your father and mother' (Exod. 20: 12, Deut. 5: 16). The Hebrew verb is *kabbēd*, a verb which means basically 'to be heavy'. Perhaps, therefore, the overtone is to treat persons with the full 'weight' of dignity which their position bears, whether a human parent or God himself. So a man of God brings to Eli Yahweh's message, 'Those who honour [*kbd*] me I will honour, and those who despise me shall be lightly esteemed' (1 Sam. 2: 30). Here we find the contrast between the 'weight' of honour due and the 'lightness' of an attitude of scorn or neglect. Perhaps the Latin word *gravitas* catches something of the nuance of this Hebrew word *kabbēd* as that which is due to a parent. However, it is not only an attitude of what we should call 'respect' that is called for, but submission to a parent's authority.

Israel's Wisdom writers[2] made a good deal of use of the father-son relationship. The Wisdom teachers themselves, in one sense, stand in *loco parentis* and address the pupils as 'my son' (e.g. Prov. 2: 1, 3: 1, etc.). But they also call repeatedly for a proper attitude of respect for and obedience to parents.

> A wise son hears his father's instruction,
> but a scoffer does not listen to rebuke. (Prov. 13: 1)

> Hearken to your father who begot you,
> and do not despise your mother when she is old. (Prov. 23: 22)

Indeed, the threats that accompany such calls can sound quite horrifying:

> The eye that mocks a father
> and scorns to obey a mother
> will be picked out by the ravens of the valley
> and eaten by vultures. (Prov. 30: 17)

This sounds a little like a distracted modern parent telling a fractious child, 'If you don't stop doing that the bogey-man will get you!' Nevertheless, discipline was clearly seen as part of a father's proper role towards his children. If God disciplines his children he is acting in a way recognised as that of any responsible and loving parent:

> My son, do not despise the LORD's discipline
> or be weary of his reproof,
> for the LORD reproves him whom he loves,
> as a father the son in whom he delights. (Prov. 3: 12f.)

Some mental reprocessing of the image of fatherhood may be necessary, then, when we adjust our sights from modern, western society, with its rather more splintered and individualistic concept of 'the family' and its more democratic view of parenthood, to that of ancient Israel. But it would be quite wrong to see Old Testament fatherhood solely in terms of autocratic and arbitrary dictatorship over children. Parents also had obligations. Clearly, paternal love was also known and seen as the natural state of things.

> As a father pitieth his children
> so the LORD pities those who fear him. (Ps. 103: 13)

Further, the responsibility for the care and protection of children is clear from imagery which is frequently used. Isaiah brings an oracle to Shebna, who had an office of responsibility in the royal household, threatening him with demotion and replacement by Eliakim. Of Eliakim it is said:

> I will . . . commit your authority to his hand, and he shall be a father to the inhabitants of Jerusalem and to the house of Judah. (Isa. 22: 20f.)

In other words, God will give him a position of special care and responsibility for the well-being of the city and its people. Job, asserting his innocence in the face of the terrible suffering which he has experienced and which his friends interpret as God's judgement, says:

> I was eyes to the blind,
> and feet to the lame,
> I was a father to the poor
> and I searched out the cause of him I did not know. (Jb. 29: 15f.)

He acted to anyone in need as a father would be expected to act towards his children. Similarly, Joseph who was appointed to be in charge of Pharaoh's affairs in Egypt, can say, '[God] has made me a father to Pharaoh and lord of all his house' (Gen. 45: 8).

An important aspect of fatherhood in the Old Testament is the relation between a father and his 'first-born' son. Several passages show the special status of the oldest, or 'first-born', and this almost always refers to the oldest son. For example, the prophet of Zechariah 12: 10 can imagine no greater grief than that of those who mourn 'for an only child, and weep bitterly over him, as one weeps over a first-born son'. Micah, thinking of the greatest sacrifice one could make, asks:

> Shall I give my first-born for my transgression,
> the fruit of my body for the sin of my soul? (Mic. 6: 7)

The greatest of all the plagues with which Yahweh could be thought to judge Egypt was that he should smite all the 'first-born in the land' (Ps. 78: 51, 105:36). In that last reference the first-born is thought to be special because he is 'the first issue of all their strength'. That is how Reuben is described in the so-called 'Blessing of Jacob':

> Reuben, you are my first-born,
> my might, and the first fruits of my strength . . . ' (Gen. 49: 3)

Partly, no doubt, because of this, and partly because of a sense of gratitude for that which 'first opened the womb' as the first sign of the blessing of fertility, special sanctity attached to the first-born. That is why all first-born were to be dedicated to God:

> You shall set apart to the LORD all that opens the womb. (Exod. 13: 15)

This applied to all, both first-born of animals and children, but, by the time of the writing of the Old Testament, the first-born child was 'redeemed', either by the offering of an animal or by money (Exod. 13: 13, 34: 19, cf. Gen. 22: 9-13, Nu. 3: 44-47). No doubt there was a gap here also between 'theology' and some 'practice', for there are hints in the Old Testament that, especially at times of crisis, children were sacrificed. So the old tradition had it that Jephthah sacrificed his daughter following his rash vow (Ju. 11: 29-40) and King Ahaz his son (II Ki. 16: 3).

Beyond this, however, what made the first-born so special was this standing in the line of inheritance. He would take over from his father the role of 'head' of the family, and he would receive a double share of the legacy of wealth that the father left. So Deuteronomy 21: 17, legislating in the case of the man who has two wives of whom one is his favourite, says that the first-born of the other wife is not be disadvantaged by his mother's fall in popularity if he was the husband's first-born:

> He shall acknowledge the first-born, the son of the disliked, by giving him a double portion of all that he has, for he is the first issue of his strength, the right of the first-born is his.

The familiar story of Jacob stealing Esau's (the first-born's) special blessing (Gen. 26) shows that the right of the first-born was the norm, even if it could be supplanted by trickery or the arbitrary whim of a father.

So a father was the provider of inheritance. Yet this was a two-way thing. For sons, particularly the first-born, were most important to the father, especially in a time when there was no lively thought of personal immortality. A man's 'name' lived on in his family, and so descendants were themselves a kind of 'legacy' to a father. They ensured the continuance of his 'name' and life in the family. How important this was is seen in the reason given for Absalom's setting up a memorial to himself near Jerusalem. He said, 'I have no son to keep my name in remembrance', and so 'he called the pillar after his own name' (I Sam. 18: 18). Similarly, the Book of Ruth records the rejoicing when a line of succession is granted to Naomi, and so to her dead husband Elimelech (Ruth 4: 17).

This is also the reason, as we have seen, for the practice of 'Levirate Marriage' in the Old Testament (discussed above in ch. 1). The first-born of such a marriage took the name of the dead husband and so perpetuated both his name and inheritance (Deut. 25: 5-10).[3]

Thus, if the father's role was to care for his children, there was also a real sense in which being father to sons was itself an enrichment. Perhaps that is why the promise of descendants figures so often as an element in the promises God is remembered as making to the patriarchs (e.g. Gen. 15: 1-6, 17: 1-5).

....

Such glimpses of what fatherhood meant in Israel, snatched here and there from the Old Testament, help us to understand better what they meant when they described God as 'Father'. Yet the Old Testament is not alone in providing us with some explanatory notes as we walk round its picture galleries. The ancient Israelites did not live in a cultural and religious vacuum. They were surrounded by other peoples, many of whom had been nations much longer than Israel had. Such people have also left us a wealth of religious texts. To examine these will enable us to see what the Israelites owed to their neighbours and, even more important, where they differed. Some of this material will be unfamiliar to many modern readers and, of course, this section can be skipped over by those whose interest is solely in what the Old Testament has to say. Yet much of this comparative material is moving and powerful in itself. And, if we look at it carefully, we shall come to understand much more about the Old Testament, just as different pictures of the same subject by different painters tell us more, not only about the subject, but about the special interest and insights of each artist.

We do not have to read far in the literature available to us before we realise that the Israelites were neither the only, nor the first people, to describe God as 'Father'. A hymn to the Moon God written in Sumerian and Akkadian opens with the following address to the deity:

> O Lord, hero of the gods, who in heaven and earth is
>   exalted in his uniqueness,
> Father Nanna, lord Anshar, hero of the gods . . .
> Father Nanna, lord of the shining crown, hero of the
>   gods . . .
> Father Nanna, who is grandly perfected in kingship,
>   hero of the gods . . .
> Begetter, merciful in his disposing, who holds in his
>   hand the life of the whole land . . .'[4]

This hymn was found on the site of ancient Nineveh in a text dating only from the 7th. century BCE (the time when Jeremiah was active in Israel) but it was copied from an older tablet whose date is unknown. We should note that the idea of the 'fatherhood' of the god is linked here with his creation of the earth and so of his all-powerful control of it, and yet also with his kindness and mercy. This forms the basis of one of the notes of praise heard later:

> Father, begetter, who looks favourably upon all living creatures.

It is interesting to note, in view of the subject of the last chapter of this book, that the deity can be addressed as both father who begets and mother who bears:

Womb that gives birth to everything, which dwells in a holy
habitation with living creatures . . . .

In Egyptian literature the god Amon-Re is addressed as 'Father
of the fathers of all the gods', in a hymn which was composed at
least as early as the first half of the second millennium BCE. The
Egyptian king could be thought of as a 'son' of the god, for
Thutmose III, (1490-1436 BCE) in a hymn of victory, describes
himself as being addressed by Amon-Re as 'My son and my
avenger'. As we shall see, the Israelites had a similar understanding of the Davidic king as God's 'son' (Ps. 2: 7). In another
inscription from the reign of Amen-hotep III (1413-1377 BCE) the
god, Amon-Re, addresses the king:

> My son, of my body, my beloved, Neb-maat-Re,
> My living image, whom my body created,
> Whom Mut, Mistress of Ishru in Thebes, the Lady of the Nine
> Bows, bore to me . . .

Much closer to the Israelites were the Canaanites, whose land
some of them had entered and which they gradually took over.
There are abundant traces in the Old Testament showing how
deeply Canaanite civilization, literature and religion influenced
Israel at many levels. In one of the Canaanite religious texts[5] King
Keret sleeps and dreams:

> And in his dream El, in his vision the father of mankind, came
> down and approached Keret, asking, 'What ails Keret that he
> weeps?'

El was the supreme god in the Canaanite pantheon. He also,
however, although father to humankind (the word is *'ādām*, as
in the Genesis creation accounts), was seen in a special sense as
father to the king. This is revealed by his suggestion that Keret
may be distressed because he is hankering after divine power:

> Does he wish for the kingship of the bull his *father*, or dominion as the *father* of humankind?

Here, both aspects of the 'fatherhood' of El are brought together, that of being father to the king and to all humankind. It is worth noting that 'Bull' was a frequent designation of El in the texts and this, doubtless, helps to explain the polemic against any form of 'calf' worship in the Old Testament (e.g. Exod. 32, I Ki. 12: 25-35, Hos. 8: 5f.).

Further evidence for the widespread concept of the god as father is provided by the form of many personal names. 'Abraham', for example, means 'Exalted Father'. Comparison with similar types of names makes it most unlikely that this is a description of Abraham himself, apart from it being an unlikely name to give to describe a new-born baby. The 'father' compound in the name (*'Āb*) almost certainly, therefore, refers to the deity. It is even clearer in a name like Abimelech which means either 'My (divine) father is king' or more probably, the *melech* compound, which in Hebrew means 'king', is the proper name of a deity, thus giving the meaning 'Melech (or Milchi) is my father.' Tradition makes the bearer of that name a king of Gerar (Gen. 20: 2), a city beyond the southern border of Israel which subsequently passed under Philistine control.[6]

More evidence that the use of such names was current outside Israel is offered by the *Tell-el-Amarna Letters*. These letters, inscribed on clay tablets, were found by chance in the 19th. century at a place now known in Arabic as Tell-el-Amarna, about two hundred miles south of Cairo on the East bank of the Nile. They date from the 14th. century BCE and consist mainly of diplomatic correspondence between kings of the city-states in the land of Canaan and surrounding areas, and the royal court of the Egyptian king Amen-hotep IV of whom they were dependants. Many of the letters contain appeals for military help against invading peoples, sometimes referred to as Habiru.[7] Four of the letters come from a Governor of Tyre called *Abi-milki*. This is almost an exact equivalent of 'Abimelech', and could be similarly rendered either 'My (divine) father is king' or, more probably, 'My (divine) father is Milki', the latter being the proper name of a deity.

Some names in the Old Testament such as Abiram ('my father is exalted'), Eliab ('my god is father'), Abiezer ('my father is help') and Abinoam ('my father is delight') suggest that, from quite early, Israel shared with the peoples of the ancient world a sense of being in a relationship of kinship with their particular deity. 'Fatherhood' is not the only relationship denoted by such names. Compounds meaning 'brother' (*Ah*) are also found in such names as Ahimelech and Ahiezer, while the name Ammiel means 'God is my kinsman'. The fact that such names occur in the earlier sources of the Old Testament, but very infrequently from the time of the exile onwards, suggests that this was a legacy from the wider social and political context from which Israel emerged.

It is not hard to imagine how such an evidently widespread concept of God could have developed. A father was thought of as the procreator, not just of his own immediate children born of his wife or wives, but of the whole family, clan or nation which traces its origins back to him. There are plenty of stories in the literature of the Ancient Near East which show how conscious people were of being the 'creation' of the gods, although these usually show awareness of the hybrid quality of human nature by speaking of a mixture of the 'divine' and 'earthy' in their make-up. The connection of creation with fatherhood is explicit in an Egyptian text from the so-called 'Shabaka Stone':

Ptah who is upon the Great Throne;
Ptah Nun, the father who begot Atum;

Interestingly, the link is made also with the female part played in birth:

Ptah-Nanuet, the mother who bore Atum.

It was, in fact, this same Ptah 'who gave birth to the gods'. Ptah thus comprises both male and female elements.

This idea, however, seems to be avoided in an earlier Egyptian *Pyramid Text* where the god Atum is spoken of as having brought about creation by an act of masturbation. His seed, thus produced, brought into being a primeval pair, Shu and Tefnut.[8]

An ancient Sumerian legend describes creation by a god, Enki. He sailed on the primordial waters to create a temple, and two lines describe his coming in this way:

> At the time when the Father sailed to the world,
> At the time when Enki sailed to the world.

In the Babylonian epic, *Enuma-Elish* (so called from its opening words which mean 'When on high'), Enki appears as Ea. Although he is here being supplanted by Marduk who creates the world by his defeat of the sea-monster Tiamat, Ea is described as the 'father' of Marduk: 'He who begot him, was Ea his father'. This line is immediately followed by a description of the role of the mother goddess: 'She who bore him was Damkina, his mother.'

The obvious link with the idea of creation, then, must have helped to furnish the very widespread concept of the deity as the divine father, although the association with the sexual act of procreation, and especially the consequent 'feminine' element in the deity, may have provided a problem for Yahwism. We shall notice shortly that the appeal to God as 'begetter' of all people is not prominent in the Old Testament allusions to him as 'father', and this may be one reason why.

Beyond the obvious link with the fact that the god(s) is, or are, seen as Creator/Father, the role of the deities in the care and protection of their people supplies another strand in the threads connecting the concepts of deity and fatherhood. We have seen an explicit reference to this in the early Mesopotamian hymn to the Moon God, *Nanna*. The personal names which speak of the deity as, in some sense, related kinsman (father, brother, and so on) must also be evidence of this element in the belief. The giving of such names must have been an expression of at least the hope, and perhaps the claim, that the ones so named would enjoy the patronage and care of the deity in a way members of a family would expect from its head.

•••••••••••••••••••

With these insights from the Old Testament and from the religious literature of Israel's neighbours into something of what fatherhood meant, how it was seen as an ideal and how it was experienced in fact, we can turn the better equipped to the use made of the picture of 'God as Father' in the Old Testament.

GOD AS FATHER

First, we should note that he is seen as father by virtue of his act of 'begetting' people as his children, by the act of creation itself. But here our first surprise awaits us. The picture is used very little to speak of God's relationship to all peoples as universal creator. The nearest approach to such a use of it comes in an extended passage from Second Isaiah. It follows his claim that God is using the Persian, Cyrus, as the instrument of his purpose for the redemption of Israel, even using the term 'anointed' (Heb. *Messiah*) of him (Isa. 44: 24, 45: 8), a term usually reserved in the Old Testament for the Davidic king. We have seen already that this aroused some resentment among the prophet's Jewish hearers who had doubts about whether God could, or would, use a Gentile Emperor in such a way. The prophet meets their objections head-on, but now we need to quote his reply more fully than we did in Chapter Two. We find that he copes with their criticisms by appealing not only to the picture of God as Craftsman, but also as Father.

> Woe to him who strives with his Maker,
> an earthen vessel with the potter!
> Does the clay say to him who fashions it, 'What are you making'?
> or 'Your work has no handles'?
> Woe to him who says to a *father*,
> 'What are you begetting?'
> or to a woman, 'With what are you in travail?'
> Thus says the LORD,
> the Holy One of Israel, and his Maker:
> 'Will you question me about *my children*,
> or command me concerning the work of my hands?
> I made the earth,
> and created man upon it;
> it was my hands that stretched out the heavens,
> and I commanded all their host.
> I have aroused him [Cyrus] in righteousness,
> and I will make straight all his ways;
> he shall build my city
> and set my exiles free . . . .' (Isa. 45: 9-13)

Here the picture of God as father is used in a context which says that he has created all people, the word 'man' being the Hebrew word *'ādām* (humankind). He is, therefore, able to use whom he will. He is universal father of all humankind by his act of creation.

Such thought is not entirely strange to the Old Testament or peculiar to this prophet. The first eleven chapters of Genesis speak of God's creation of *'ādām* (humankind), and of his relationship of care and providence towards all. This is expressed most clearly in the account of the Covenant with Noah given by the Priestly writer (Gen. 9: 1-7), but also in the Yahwist's view of this Covenant (Gen. 8: 21f.). It is the covenant to which Jesus referred when he pointed out that God sends his sun and rain on the good and the bad (Mt. 5: 45).

It is difficult to be sure of the date of such ideas. Genesis chapters 1-11 in their final, canonical form, serve as Prologue to the story of redemption in God's call to Abraham and his purposes for Israel, described from Genesis 12 onwards. The 'schema' of Genesis 1-11 and its careful dovetailing with the patriarchal stories to follow, is probably the work of the Priestly writer who worked in the exile—interestingly, the same period as that in which the prophet 'Second Isaiah' worked. But if that is the date of the final composition, it is impossible to know to what extent they were drawing on older ideas. Possibly, it was the experience of the exile that first drove some in Israel to ask questions about the relationship of their God, Yahweh, to *all* the peoples of the earth. But we must be careful here, for there is plenty of evidence in the prophets, (Amos and Isaiah are two examples), let alone in Israel's psalmody, to show that they thought of Yahweh as creator and universal king whose authority extended to all places and over all nations, even over other 'gods'. All of this was from times well before the exile.

Nevertheless, those pre-exilic and exilic sources do not use the picture of God as universal Father in the context of *creation*. Indeed, apart from the passage in Isaiah 45, already cited, the picture of God as the father who 'begets' his children is used exclusively in the context of his purpose for *Israel*. This is how we have to understand Malachi's rhetorical question:

> Have we not all one father?
> Has not one God created us? (Mal. 2: 10)

It is possible that the reference here to 'one father' is to Abraham, and some commentators have so understood it. But the 'parallelism' of Hebrew poetry (a device whereby, instead of a rhyme of words, a 'rhyme' or 'parallelism' of ideas is created by expressing the same thought in different ways in successive lines) makes it most likely that the reference is to God. But the fact that Malachi is thinking of God as 'father' by his creation of *Israel*, rather than *all people*, is clear from what follows. He charges members of the post-exilic community with faithlessness to each other in their dealings within their own community. They are denying their family relationship as 'brothers' by their descent from a common parenthood, that of God their 'father'. Such conduct he describes as 'profaning the covenant of our fathers' (v. 10).

Indeed, some Old Testament scholars believe that the reference to God as 'creator' or 'begetter' of Israel here refers to the tradition of the forming of the covenant relationship between Yahweh and Israel on Mount Sinai. Further, some have argued that the 'father-son' terminology is characteristic of covenant and treaty language, not only in Israel's own idea of a religious covenant between herself and Yahweh, but also more widely in the language used in treaty covenants of a more political nature between nations in the Ancient Near East. In the *Tell-el-Amarna Letters*, to which reference has already been made, Abdu-heba, governor of Jerusalem, writes to the king of Egypt to call for help against attackers, and he bases his appeal on their treaty relationship by signing himself, 'Thy servant, *thy son* am I'. In exactly the same way in the Old Testament, King Ahaz of Judah, pressed by the combined forces of Syria and the northern kingdom of Israel, appeals to the King of Assyria and says of himself, 'I am your servant *and your son*' (II Ki. 16: 7). A similar thought is expressed in Deuteronomy with its very strong emphasis on the covenant relationship. In a passage chiding the Israelites for their disobedience we read:

> Do you thus requite the LORD,
> you foolish and senseless people?
> Is he not your father, who created you,
> who made you and established you?' (Deut. 32: 6)

In the Deuteronomic tradition there is no doubt at what point in their history God 'made' and 'established' them as his children. He did so when he brought them out of Egypt and entered into a covenant relationship with them (e.g. Deut. 7: 6-11). Indeed, the very word to 'create' in Deuteronomy 32: 6 is a word that often means 'to buy' or 'acquire'. It can mean simply to 'create', for it is used in Genesis 14: 19,22 to describe God as 'maker' of heaven and earth. But elsewhere it is used of God's redeeming his people, as in Exodus 15: 16 in the 'Song of the Sea'. Depicting the fear of surrounding peoples as God delivered his people, the song records:

> Terror and dread fell upon them;
> because of the greatness of thy arm, they are as still
>   as a stone,
> till thy people, O LORD, pass by,
> till the people pass by whom thou hast *purchased*.

Deuteronomy itself uses the word ('create' or 'purchase') elsewhere in a mocking picture of God's judgement as a reversal of his original act of salvation. Warning the people of what is to come if they do not keep the conditions of the covenant, it says:

> And the LORD will bring you back in ships to Egypt, a journey which I promised you should never make again; and there you shall offer yourselves for sale to your enemies as male and female slaves, but no money *will buy you*. (Deut. 28: 68)

At every point the salvation story is reversed. Instead of coming out of Egypt they will go back into it; instead of being freed they will return to slavery. Where once God 'bought' them, now no one will be found who thinks them worth purchase.

This emphasis on God's saving action in history, thinking of the 'making' or begetting of his children as a historic act of redemption and purchase, may well have eased what might have been a problem for the prophets and the Deuteronomists. If God is 'father' to Israel, then the act of 'begetting' his children might well have been thought to involve some female deity who 'bore' them. We have seen how, in other Ancient Near Eastern mythology, human beings were seen in some way as the product of sexual activity among the gods. This would be unthinkable for the more sophisticated theologians of Yahwism, however it might have been understood at popular levels. The word most often used for the action of 'begetting' in the Old Testament is the Hebrew verb *yāladh*. An ambiguity can attach to it, however, for it is used both of the role of the father in conception and the action of the mother in 'bearing' or 'bringing forth' the child.

Something of this ambivalence can be seen in a rhetorical question posed in Jeremiah 30: 6. Speaking of the terror which is afflicting the community in a time of judgement, a time of unnatural terror, the prophet asks:

> Ask now, and see,
> Can a man bear a child?

The point of the question is that men in the community pale and agonized as though they were women in the act of delivering a baby. Yet the verb *yāladh*, which occurs here, is often used of the man's part in conception. So the Wisdom teachers can say, 'Listen to your father who begot (*yāladh*) you' (Prov. 23: 22). The same verb appears repeatedly in the genealogical lists, often being rendered in modern English versions by 'X was the father of Y'. In Zechariah 13: 3 it is used of both parents:

> And if any one again appears as a prophet, his father and mother who bore him [the plural participle is used] will say to him, 'You shall not live . . .'

The same verb is used in Deuteronomy of God's part in bringing Israel into being. Again criticizing the people for their disloyalty to God it says:

> You were unmindful of the Rock that begot you,
> and you forgot the God who gave you birth. (Det. 32: 18)

The first line uses the verb *yāladh*, but the second uses a verb (*ḥûl*) usually much more explicitly associated with the woman's act of childbirth.

So, in metaphor at least, God is seen as exercising both a father's and mother's role in 'begetting'. This will be of interest when, later, we consider the 'feminine' aspect of God in the Old Testament. For the present we may simply observe that it is this very ambivalence in the idea which might lead to an association of Yahweh with the fertility cults and the symbolism of sacral marriage which characterised the nature religion of some neighbouring people. Perhaps it is the presence of this danger that leads to an emphasis in at least some traditions in the Old Testament (e.g. some prophets and the Deuteronomists) on Yahweh's act of begetting Israel as being linked firmly with his historical act of deliverance from Egypt. According to such traditions, Sinai was Israel's maternity ward.

At this point we must note a particular line that branches off from the main track of the tradition that Yahweh is Israel's father. To this point we have seen the faith expressed that Yahweh is the father of all Israel and all Israel is his son. There developed also, however, a doctrine that a special father-son relationship existed between God and the king of the Davidic line who ruled in Jerusalem. The clearest expression of this occurs in Psalm 2, which is a psalm that was used, either at the coronation of such a king, or at some anniversary event celebrating and re-affirming that coronation. The king is there described as Yahweh's 'anointed' (Heb. *messiah*, v. 2). It carries the assurance that Yahweh has established this king in his rule:

> 'I have set my king
> on Zion, my holy hill'. (v. 3)

That verse indicates how closely the 'Davidic covenant' and 'Zion' traditions intertwined with each other. The Davidic king is of God's appointing and enthroning. Zion, i.e. Jerusalem (the name of the temple mount giving its name symbolically to the whole city), is Yahweh's own city, his 'resting place for ever' (Ps. 132: 14), and the place which he will defend against all assaults from enemies (Ps. 46: 5, 7, 11). Here, in Psalm 2, the Davidic king is also promised divine assistance against his enemies. His cause is Yahweh's cause. Indeed, Yahweh himself has uttered a solemn 'decree' (the Hebrew word is often translated as 'statute' and is one of the terms used to describe the immutable divine law):

GOD AS FATHER

> He said to me, 'You are my son,
> Today I have begotten you' [Heb. *yāladh*].

This understanding of the role of the Davidic king, and this use of the father-son imagery to describe it, also springs from 'covenant' theology. In this case, however, it is not the covenant with the whole nation made at *Sinai*, but the covenant it was believed (at least by some) that Yahweh had made with *David* and his successors and which had been conveyed to David by the prophet Nathan (II Sam. 7: 4-17). We shall have to explore all this more fully when we come to consider the Old Testament image of God as 'King'. Now we need merely note it as a divergent tradition within the Old Testament.

It may seem strange to the non-specialist reader of the Old Testament that we cannot be sure which of these traditions—on the one hand the Sinaitic covenant tradition which was more strongly maintained in the north, and on the other hand the 'David-Zion' tradition more closely associated with the south—was the 'original' Yahwistic tradition. Did the David-Zion tradition diverge from an older Sinai tradition as a later variant of it? Or did the Sinaitic covenant tradition represent a northern reaction against the David-Zion tradition because the northerners saw it being used to bolster southern claims to leadership? Some prophets certainly rejected the 'Zion' theology. But our sources are all so much later than the events they narrate and all so represent particular viewpoints, that reconstruction of the early period of Israel's history is a very hazardous enterprise.

It seems more probable on the whole that the David-Zion theology was introduced into more traditional Yahwism as a new element which always sat rather awkwardly with the older. But we cannot be sure. However, whichever historical answer we arrive at, the issue does not really affect our study of the picture of 'Father'. The use of the father-son imagery in the Davidic covenant tradition, a use we have already seen to have been current in the understanding of monarchy elsewhere in the Ancient Near East, brings little that is new into it. It does see God's relationship as father being mediated to the nation through the king rather than being directly with the community as a whole. But either way, Yahweh is still father to the covenant community, whether that community is seen to be represented before God by the king or not.

We may thus summarise the aspect of 'creating-begetting' in the Old Testament picture of God as father by saying that in most of the forms in which it appears, it presents God as the Founder and Ancestor, the 'Begetter' of the 'clan' of the Israelite nation. This 'begetting' took place in his deliverance of the nation from slavery in Egypt and in the founding of the Covenant by which he made them his own. In this, the relationship owes as much to the initiative of divine grace as our human life owes to the initiative of our human father. This is where the real emphasis in the Old Testament picture of God as father and 'begetter' lies. The picture is used very little to make the point that by his act of universal creation of humankind God is in some sense 'father' to all peoples. It is used not at all to suggest that Israel is somehow the produce of Yahweh's sexual activity. This double contrast with much of the literature of Israel's neighbours is most informative.

The theme of Yahweh's care as father for his children evokes some of the finest poetry in the Old Testament, whether it be the words of prophets or the language of prayer and devotion in Israel's psalmody. Perhaps the most daring is Hosea who compares God's care for the nation since its infancy in Egypt with that of a parent proudly and tenderly guiding his child to its first steps with the aid of a walking harness:

> When Israel was a child, I loved him,
> and out of Egypt I called my son . . .
> it was I who taught Ephraim to walk,
> I took them up in my arms . . .
> I led them with cords of compassion,
> with the bands of love. (Hos. 11: 1, 3f.)

This is contrasted with Israel's continued waywardness which will bring down God's judgement. Yet Hosea pictures that tension all parents know between wrath and the ties of love, as existing even within God himself. After his outburst of anger he continues:

> How can I give you up, O Ephraim?
> How can I hand you over, O Israel? . . .
> My heart recoils within me,
> my compassion grows warm and tender.
> I will not execute my fierce anger,
> I will not again destroy Ephraim;
> for I am God and not man . . . (Hos. 11: 8f.)

It is true that a slight ambiguity attaches to this last passage, since the Hebrew word rendered 'How' at the beginning of the first two lines can introduce either an exclamation or a question. Nevertheless, the context suggests that Hosea has discerned something of the tension between judgement and love which can be resolved only by forgiving grace, and this provides a glimpse of an agony which is to appear much later in fuller form in the New Testament.

The Book of Jeremiah, which echoes many of the themes of Hosea and uses much of his language, finds in the thought of the fatherhood of God hope for the future. It pictures the return of the exiles to their own land again, the idea of a 'return' having a double edge. It signifies both a geographical return from Babylon and a 'return' in repentance to Yahweh.

> With weeping they shall come,
> and with cries for grace I will lead them back,[9]
> I will make them walk by brooks of water,
> in a straight path in which they shall not stumble;
> for I am a father to Israel,
> and Ephraim is my first-born. (Jer. 31: 9)

God's concern for his exiled people was known to them from the traditions of the slavery of their fathers in Egypt. God intervened then on their behalf. He instructed Moses:

> You shall say to Pharaoh,
> "Thus says the LORD, 'Israel is my first-born son . . .
> Let my son go that he may serve me.'" (Exod. 4: 22-23)

The prophet of the latest chapters of the Book of Isaiah sees the care of God for his children as a father forming the basis of their prayer in the distress of the exile:

> For thou art our Father,
> though Abraham does not know us
> and Israel does not acknowledge us;
> [i.e. they have proved unworthy of their past.]
> thou, O LORD, art our Father,
> our Redeemer from of old is thy name. (Isa. 63: 16)

Again, in the next chapter, the people are portrayed as casting themselves on the fatherly care and power of the one who created them:

> Yet, O LORD, thou art our Father;
> we are the clay, and thou art the potter;
> we are all the work of thy hand.
> Be not exceedingly angry, O LORD,
> and remember not iniquity for ever. (Isa. 64: 8f.)

Such confidence in God's fatherhood is expressed in the language of Israel's worship. The care and protection of God as father to the weak and helpless is the theme of Ps. 68: 5:

> Father of the fatherless and protector of widows
> is God in his holy habitation.

Indeed, his fatherly care transcends the claims and ties of human parenthood:

> If my father and my mother should forsake me, then
> the LORD would gather me up in his care. (Ps. 27: 10)

All these passages show how the concept of God as father could inspire trust in times of despair, hope in experience of failure, gratitude for past love and confidence for an uncertain future. The concept crosses the boundaries of literary types, appearing in Laments, Hymns of Praise, Expressions of Confidence and Prophetic Exhortations. In them we hear the heartbeat of religious experience and devotion. Equally they illustrate what I drew attention to earlier as the two-way, or what we might call the 'dual-carriageway', character of these pictures. Human experience of the parent-child relationship illuminates the nature of God and of his relationship with his people. But they also throw

GOD AS FATHER

light on the nature of human parenthood and what, ideally, that should be.

It was also said earlier that there is an 'existential' dimension to these pictures. They are 'dual-carriageways' also in that they convey not only God's care and action on behalf of his children, but summon his children to their proper response of filial trust and obedience to such a father. This element recurs frequently in the Old Testament, especially among the prophets. We have already heard Malachi:

> A son honours his father, and a servant his master,
> If then I am a father, where is my honour?
> And if I am a master, where is my fear? (Mal. 1: 6)

The 'honour' for the father is that called for towards parents in the Decalogue: 'Honour your father and your mother' (Exod. 20: 12, cf. Deut. 5: 16). If that is our due to earthly parents, how much more should it characterise our response to God, our heavenly father? That seems to be the thrust of Malachi's message.

The hypocrisy of calling God 'father' in the language of prayer and worship, but refusing the obedience a father expects from his children, is the theme of these words of Jeremiah:

> Have you not just now called to me,
> 'My father, thou art the friend of my youth—
> will he be indignant to the end?'
> Behold, you have spoken,
> but you have done all the evil that you could. (Jer. 3: 4f.)

For Jeremiah, an equal enormity is the worship of the gods of other cults. How absurd for those who claim Yahweh as 'father' to be the very ones:

> who say to a tree, 'You are my father,'
> and to a stone, 'You gave me birth.'
> For they have turned their back to me,
> and not their face.
> But in the time of their trouble they say,
> 'Arise and save us!' (Jer. 2: 27)

Such a biting edge to the use of the picture of God as father delivers it from the bluntness of a merely soft sentimentality. God is not just the universal escape-figure of Freudian hypothesis. In the manner of fathers in ancient Near Eastern societies he is a figure of some awe, power and authority who exists, not only to provide for his children what they want, but to claim from them what his status as their father demands and their duties as his children should offer.

This double aspect to fatherhood, that which God as father *gives*, but that which as father he *expects*, is to be found also in the status of children as 'heirs'. That God, as father, gives an 'inheritance' to his children, is a frequent theme in the Old Testament. The land plays a prominent part in this theme. All the traditions see the promise of land as being a vital part of the covenant with the patriarchs (e.g. Gen. 15: 7, 17: 8, 26: 3, 28: 13, 35: 12, etc.). The Deuteronomic tradition especially stresses that the land of Canaan was God's gift, his 'inheritance' to Israel (e.g. Deut. 4: 21). Jeremiah portrays God as saying to the nation:

> I thought
> how I would set you among my sons,
> and give you a pleasant land,
> a heritage most beauteous of all nations.
> And I thought you would call me, 'My Father',
> and would not turn from following me. (Jer. 3: 19)

This is also implicit in the assertion that Israel is God's 'first-born' and therefore due for a special 'inheritance' from her father:

> for I am a father to Israel,
> and Ephraim is my first-born. (Jer. 31: 9)

Membership of the covenant people who have been given this land is itself an 'inheritance' from God. So Job, pleading his innocence by a series of negatives, listing those evil things he has not done, can say:

> I have made a covenant with my eyes;
> how then could I look upon a virgin?

What would be my portion from God above,
and my heritage from the Almighty on high? (Job 31: 1f.)

In other words, he would no longer be fit to be a member of the community of God's 'family'.

In the Deuteronomistic tradition, the division of each part of the land to the individual tribes is spoken of as that part which was 'the inheritance of the tribe of X'. The law dealing with the Levitical priests, who were to own no land, uses an interesting phrase:

> You [the Aaronite/Levitical priests] shall have no inheritance in their land, neither shall you have any portion among them; I am your portion and your inheritance among the people of Israel. (Nu. 18: 20)

This means that they will receive their living from the tithes given by all Israelites towards the upkeep of the temple, as the following verse makes clear. But it shows also how the land, its produce and care for all material needs, are the 'inheritance' God, as father, gives to his covenant people. As his first-born, Israel has received a double blessing compared with all the other nations. This is precisely the promise whose renewal is promised after the exile:

> Instead of your shame you shall have a double portion,
> instead of dishonour you shall rejoice in your lot;
> therefore in your land you shall possess a double portion;
> yours shall be everlasting joy. (Isa. 61: 7, cf. Zech. 9: 12)

Yet there is a remarkable twist to this in the Old Testament. For, in addition to the thought of God as father giving his children, Israel his first-born, a special inheritance, Israel is itself said to be *God's* own inheritance. Children bring an especial joy and pride to parents. Indeed, Psalm 127 makes this explicit:

> Lo, sons are a heritage from the LORD,
> the fruit of the womb a reward.
> Like arrows in the hand of a warrior
> are the sons of one's youth.

> Happy is the man who has his quiver full of them!
> He shall not be put to shame
> when he speaks with his enemies in the gate. (vv. 3-5)

We have observed already that descendants were seen to safeguard the perpetuation of a man's 'name' when there was no concept of a personal immortality. To this, Psalm 127 adds the thought that 'sons' safeguard the family and its possessions, just as arrows are carried for self-defence. The strength of the family is seen also at 'the gate', the Hebrew equivalent of a court of law. It was in the open area just inside a city gate that elders would meet to decide matters of concern for the community, and this included legal disputes between its citizens. So often, those without the protection afforded by a strong family, the poor, the widow and the orphan, were defenceless at law against the powerful and the wealthy who could try to rob a family of its inheritance by bribery or violence. The prophets denounce this often enough to show that it happened (e.g. Amos 5: 10-12).

In view of the idea that his family, Israel, is God's own heritage, the following passage from Deuteronomy is particularly interesting:

> When the Most High gave to the nations their inheritance,
> when he separated the sons of men,
> he fixed the bounds of the peoples
> according to the number of the sons of God.
> For the LORD's portion is his people,
> Jacob his allotted heritage. (Deut. 32: 8f.)

The thought is strange to us. It proposes that God originally destined land for each nation on earth, just as he gave the land of Canaan to Israel as their 'inheritance'. Each nation, however, was given its heavenly protector, 'sons of God' here meaning heavenly beings who act as God's servants and who, on occasion, form a kind of 'Council of Heaven' whom God consults.[10] Whatever difficulties the concept raises, however, the main thought is clear enough for our present purposes. Israel is Yahweh's own special 'heritage' which he keeps for himself. Nor is this an isolated instance of the idea. It was a theme of the nation's worship:

> The LORD is the strength of his people,
> he is the saving refuge of his anointed.
> O save thy people, and bless thy heritage,
> be thou their shepherd, and carry them for ever. (Ps. 28: 8f.)

It occurs in the prophetic literature, even if in a 'negative' context:

> I have forsaken my house,
> I have abandoned my heritage;
> I have given the beloved of my soul
> into the hands of her enemies.
> My heritage has become to me like a lion in the forest,
> she has lifted up her voice against me. (Jer. 12: 7f.)

Indeed, the bitterness of that cry sounds the distorted echo of what Israel as God's heritage meant to him. He looked to them for a response of love, trust and obedience. He hoped to see his purposes fulfilled through them as a father's ambitions centre on the lives of his children. At least one persistent strand of thought runs through the Old Testament, showing that God looked for his 'children', Israel, to be the means of revelation of his own nature on a world-wide scale. As early as when Abraham is called the promise is given, 'By you shall all the families of the earth bless themselves' (Gen. 12: 3). This means that God will so bless Abraham and his descendants that all nations will use him as a 'yardstick' of blessing: 'May you be blessed as Abraham has been blessed' will become a universal blessing. Implicit in that must surely be some universal acknowledgement of Yahweh as the source of that blessing. Second Isaiah sounds this theme repeatedly:

> I am the LORD, I have called you in righteousness . . .
> I have given you as a covenant to the people,
> a light to the nations,
> to open eyes that are blind,
> to bring out prisoners from the dungeon,
> from the prison those who sit in darkness. (Isa. 42: 6f.)

So does God, as father, hope that his purposes will find expression and fulfilment through his 'children'. Law and Prophets both call for that life of moral obedience which will reflect something of God's nature. In the Book of the Covenant[11] God calls for compassion for the immigrant and the poor, the widow and the orphan, even the debtor, 'because I am compassionate' (Exod. 22: 21-27). This is the sense in which Israel as God's 'son' is 'called by his name', as Second Isaiah says of the people:

> But now thus says the LORD,
> he who created you, O Jacob,
> he who formed you, O Israel:
> Fear not, for I have redeemed you;
> I have called you by name, you are mine. (Isa. 43: 1)

That is why he had to judge his people, according to Ezekiel, because by their misconduct, they had 'profaned my holy name among the nations' (Ezek. 36: 21). Yet, for the sake of that very name, the ultimate conviction of Ezekiel is that God will forgive, cleanse, renew and restore his people (vv. 22-32).

The Old Testament picture of God as father, then, proves to be a rich one with many varied strata of meaning and significance. It at once precludes sentimentality and presumption, but encourages the call for filial love and obedience. It shows how God took the initiative in bringing his 'children' into being by his great redemptive act in the Exodus. It portrays a God whose care and protection of his children can be relied on for all who 'honour' him as any parent must be honoured. It shows how judgement may fall, but that it falls within an ultimate concern of love and desire to make his people fit the dictum, 'Like father, like son'. At the deepest level it daringly says that there are points of contact between God and the family relationships of those created 'in his image'. The most startling feature of it is that it portrays a God who is not self-sufficient. Like any father, he provides for his children in care and by inheritance. But his children are also his inheritance, without whose response he is self-confessedly incomplete.

NOTES TO CHAPTER THREE

1. See R. de Vaux, *Ancient Israel: Its Life and Institutions*, English translation by John McHugh, London, 1961, p.20.

2. The term often given to those who produced the books of Proverbs, Job, Ecclesiastes, the Song of Songs, The Wisdom of Solomon and Ecclesiasticus. This genre of literature is usually referred to as 'The Wisdom Literature'. For an account of it see J.L. Crenshaw, *Old Testament Wisdom: An Introduction*, London, 1982.

3. The passage in Deuteronomy, as we have seen, legislates only for brothers living together in the same house, but there are suggestions elsewhere (e.g. the Book of Ruth) that it once extended also, not only to brothers living separately but, where there were no brothers, to the next nearest male kinsman.

4. Unless otherwise stated, all translations of the ancient near eastern literature are those to be found in J.B. Pritchard, (ed.), *Ancient Near Eastern Texts relating to the Old Testament*, (3rd. ed. with supplement), Princeton, 1969.

5. *Keret*, i 36ff. For a translation and commentary of this text see G.R. Driver, *Canaanite Myths and Legends,* Edinburgh, 1956. These texts, dating from the 14th. century BCE, are known as the Ugaritic Texts because they were discovered at Ugarit, whose modern name is Ras Shamra. This site is situated near the Mediterranean coast in the extreme north west of Canaan in what is modern Syria and was then a region under the control of Phoenicia.

6. The Philistines were sea-people from the Aegean Islands who, themselves under pressure from invading peoples, settled all round the eastern and southern Mediterranean sea-board in the 12th. century BCE. Those who figure most prominently in the Old Testament were repulsed by Egypt and settled in the south-western corner of the country we now know as Palestine. They were organised around five cities, Ashdod, Ashkelon, Ekron, Gath and Gaza. Today this area is often referred to as 'the Gaza Strip'.

7. The question of whether at least some of those referred to had any relation to the 'Hebrews' and their incursions into this area is a very complicated historical issue which does not concern us here.

8. An interesting account of many of the ancient near eastern creation myths is given by S.G.F. Brandon in *Creation Legends of the Ancient Near East*, London, 1963.

9. This is often emended on the basis of the Versions to read 'with consolations I will bring them back' (so RSV). But the Hebrew text makes good sense. It implies that the exiles will return, not only physically to the land, but that they will return 'spiritually' to God, their father, in gratitude for his love.

10. The Hebrew text here reads 'sons of Israel' in place of 'sons of God'. The RSV is certainly right to replace this meaningless phrase on the basis of the text preserved in other versions. Perhaps it was changed to avoid any suggestion of polytheism. The idea of each nation having its heavenly 'protector' recurs in the Book of Daniel, probably the latest book in the Old Testament. For a discussion of the Old Testament idea of 'The Council of Heaven' see R.N. Whybray, *The Heavenly Counsellor in Isaiah xl 13-14*, Cambridge, 1971.

11. The name given to the law code to be found in Exodus 20: 22- 23: 33.

IV

GOD AS HUMAN

Twice in the Book of Psalms there occur words scornfully contrasting the images which represent the gods of other nations with Yahweh, the God of Israel.

> Our God is in the heavens;
> he does whatever he pleases.
> Their idols are silver and gold,
> the work of men's hands.
> They have mouths, but do not speak;
> eyes, but do not see.
> They have ears, but do not hear;
> noses, but do not smell.
> They have hands, but do not feel;
> feet, but do not walk;
> and they do not make a sound in their throat.
> (Ps. 115: 3-7)

Similar words, with just a few variations, occur in Psalm 135: 15-17. The implications are clear. By contrast, Yahweh is not without the 'human' qualities these other gods lack, but is supreme in possessing them. The repetition of the lines in two different psalms may indicate that they formed part of Israel's liturgical tradition, perhaps some point in the covenant worship of Yahweh where the worship of other gods was renounced.

Their context in Psalm 115 is significant. It is a hymn in praise of Yahweh's *power*. It seems to be set after some crisis which had led to the foreign nations asking 'Where is their god?' (v. 2)

Nevertheless, faith in Yahweh's constant devotion (v. 1), his constant help in past times of need (vv. 9-12a), and his cosmic rule in the heavens which results in his giving people the earth with all its creatures, and all its resources to sustain life (v. 16), lead to an assurance of his help (vv. 12b-15). Indeed, so certain are they of his deliverance from 'death' to 'life' that they know they will be able to praise him in the future (vv. 17f.). Thus a passage which is so strongly anthropomorphic leads, not to the limiting of the thought of God's power, but its enhancement.

Of course, every one of the pictures of God we are examining, portrays him in human terms. But in this chapter we shall be looking especially at the particular attribution of human faculties and characteristics to God. It is instructive to see how the various 'human' characteristics, denied in Psalms 115 and 135 to the other gods, are spoken of elsewhere in the Old Testament in connection with Yahweh.

'They have mouths, but do not speak.' The thought that Yahweh 'speaks' is fundamental to the Old Testament. He is a God who communicates himself to human beings. But, more than that, he is the god of power who creates life and brings his purposes to pass by his word. In the Priestly Writer's account of creation in Gen. 1: 1-2: 4a we read of each stage of creation, 'And God said, "Let there be". . . and there was.' (Gen. 1: 3,6,9,11,14,20,24,26). Another writer of the time of the Babylonian exile, Second Isaiah, expresses the same truth poetically as he speaks for God:

> For as the rain and the snow come down from heaven,
> and return not thither but water the earth,
> making it bring forth and sprout,
> giving seed to the sower and bread to the eater,
> so shall my word be that goes forth from my mouth;
> it shall not return to me empty,
> but it shall accomplish that which I purpose,
> and prosper in the thing for which I sent it. (Isa. 55: 10f.)

It is important to see that this 'word' of God is effective and creative and not just declarative. This is true of the word God speaks to the prophets. When they begin their oracles with the messenger formula, 'Thus says Yahweh . . .', as they so often do, or conclude it with the statement 'Oracle of Yahweh' they are not merely announcing his intention which they believe he has revealed to them. God himself is present in and active through that word, initiating the process by which his sovereign purpose is worked out. For example, when God speaks to the boy Samuel after the story of his repeated call during the night in the temple, the 'word' of the prophecy is:

> Behold, I am about to do a thing in Israel, at which the two ears of every one that hears it will tingle. On that day I will fulfil against Eli all that I have spoken concerning his house from beginning to end.
> (I Sam. 3: 11)

Or, as later God says to the prophet Ezekiel:

> But I the LORD will speak the word which I will speak, and it will be performed. (Ezek. 12: 25)

The Deuteronomists especially stress this aspect of prophecy. One test of the false prophet is that:

> ... when a prophet speaks in the name of the LORD, if the word does not come to pass or come true, that is a word which the LORD has not spoken. (Deut. 18: 22)

A true prophetic word achieves that of which it speaks. The 'Deuteronomistic History' shows how this works out in the history of Israel. History is a schema of prophetic word and its fulfilment. So, for example, Ahijah, a prophet from Shiloh, addresses Jeroboam with the prophecy:

> For thus says the LORD, the God of Israel, 'Behold, I am about to tear the kingdom from the hand of Solomon, and will give you ten tribes... (I Ki. 11: 31)

Later, when the history narrates the obstinacy of Rehoboam of Judah in refusing the demands of the northern Israelites, an obstinacy which leads to the breach between the two kingdoms of north and south, we read:

> So the king did not hearken to the people; for it was a turn of affairs brought about by the LORD that he might fulfil his word which the LORD spoke by Ahijah the Shilonite to Jeroboam the son of Nebat. (I Ki. 12: 15)

So the fact that Yahweh 'has a mouth and speaks' testifies to his sovereign power over creation and his lordship of history. He also speaks in the words of the law whose commandments are given in love to guide his people on the right path. This is what the Psalmist had in mind when he exclaimed in joy,

> Thy word is a lamp to my feet
> and a light to my path. (Ps. 119: 105)

In addition, the words of the 'Wise' are also seen as God's gift, so that it can be said of Ahitophel:

> Now in those days the counsel which Ahitophel gave was as if one consulted the oracle of God. (II Sam. 16: 23)

Indeed, the teaching of the wise is as much a gift from God as the oracles of the prophets:

> For the LORD gives wisdom;
> from his mouth comes knowledge and understanding. (Prov. 2: 6)

Like his speaking, the truth that Yahweh has 'eyes' so that he can 'see' is also regarded as a feature of his saving power and omniscience. *'They have eyes, but see not'* says the writer of Psalm 115 in mockery of the foreign gods. But God 'watches' over his people in care and protection:

> The eyes of the LORD are towards the righteous. (Ps. 34: 16).

Yet, equally, no evil or oppression escapes his attention:

> Behold, the eyes of the Lord GOD are upon the sinful kingdom, and I will destroy it from the surface of the ground. (Amos 9: 8)

The fact that this capacity underlines the sovereignty of God is stressed in another Psalm:

> The LORD looks down from heaven,
> he sees all the sons of men;
> from where he sits enthroned he looks forth
> on all the inhabitants of the earth,
> he who fashions the hearts of them all,
> and observes all their deeds. (Ps. 33: 13-15)

A remarkable example of this is Ezekiel's vision of God recorded in the first chapter of the book. It is a highly complex and obscure chapter which undoubtedly has been much expanded, but in many ways it echoes Isaiah's vision of God on his throne in the Jerusalem temple. Ezekiel's vision comes to the prophet away in Babylon and God is seated on a throne-chariot borne by four living creatures, each having four faces. The thrust seems to be that all parts of the earth are open to God's presence and God's sight, a fact which has been underlined by a later glossator who has added the detail that the rims of the chariot wheels were full of eyes (Ezek. 1: 18).

Not surprisingly this confidence inspires much of Israel's prayer in times of need. The imperative of the verb 'to see' or its equivalent, recurs in the Psalms with great frequency. Typical is Psalm 80: 14-15:

> Turn again, O God of hosts!
> Look down from heaven, and see.

Equally, it is the source of joyful praise upon deliverance:

> I will rejoice and be glad for thy steadfast love,
> because thou hast seen my affliction,
> thou hast taken heed of my adversities . . . (Ps. 31: 7)

In exactly the same way the fact that God 'hears' the cry of the oppressed is the cause of both praise and prayer. So the Psalmist is confident that Yahweh has an 'ear'. Unlike the other gods who *'have ears, but do not hear'*,

'O LORD, thou wilt hear the desire of the meek;
thou wilt strengthen their heart, thou wilt incline thine ear
to do justice to the fatherless and the oppressed,
so that man who is of the earth
may strike terror no more. (Ps. 10: 17f.)

And the worshipper who has experienced God's deliverance can say:

In my distress I called upon the LORD;
to my God I cried for help.
From his temple he heard my voice,
and my cry reached his ears. (Ps. 18: 6)

The 'ear' and the 'hand' of Yahweh are mentioned in an oracle in Isaiah 59: 1 (cf. Ps.115: 7 *'They have hands, but do not feel'*):

Behold, the LORD's hand is not shortened,
that it cannot save,
or his ear dull, that it cannot hear.

Most scholars believe that much of Isaiah chapters 56-66 stems from a time after the return from the exile. Yet much in them appears to take up thoughts and words of Second Isaiah, perhaps to re-apply them in the new situation. So the words in 59: 1 echo a promise of the exilic prophet:

Is my hand shortened, that it cannot redeem?
Or have I no power to deliver?' (Isa. 50: 2b)

The returned exiles must have been wondering if that promise was to prove true or not. Return seemed only to mean exchanging one set of troubles for another. This prophet assures them that the contrast between divine promise and human experience is due, not to a failure of God's power, but to their sinfulness (vv. 2ff.).

The 'hand' in the Old Testament is a symbol for 'power'. In the Hebrew idiom, to give someone 'into the hand of' another is to deliver them to his power. So the men of Israel call on Gideon to rule over them, saying, 'for you have delivered us out of the hand of the Midianites' meaning, 'you have delivered us from their control' (Ju. 8: 27). It can also mean the opposite. When, according to the narrator, 'the people of Israel did what was evil in the sight of the LORD', then God 'gave them into the hand of the Philistines for forty years' (Ju. 13: 1). It is used, as we have seen, by Second Isaiah, when God asks:

> Is my hand shortened, that it cannot redeem?
> Or have I no power to deliver? (Isa. 50: 2b)

So the great foundation event of God's salvation of his people, Israel, is often referred to in terms such as these:

> ... the LORD brought us out of Egypt with a mighty hand. (Deut. 6: 21)

The Psalmist can say:

> Into thy hand I commit my spirit,
> thou hast redeemed me, O LORD, faithful God. (Ps. 31: 5-6)

No doubt the reference in Psalm 115 to the gods who *'have noses, but do not smell'* is an ironic reference to the futility of offering sacrifices to them. One is reminded of the bold anthropomorphic account of the Flood. According to the 'Yahwistic' source (see ch. 2, n.1) Noah, to celebrate his safe arrival on dry ground, offered a sacrifice.

> And when the LORD smelled the pleasing odour, the LORD said in his heart, 'I will never again curse the ground because of man ....' (Gen. 8: 21)

Thus God, because he is the living God, constantly renews the relationship between humanity and himself by means of the expiatory sacrifices. He responds in grace and forgiveness to the sincere approach of the worshipper. Sacrifices to dead gods, represented by images of wood and metal, are pointless. It is equally pointless to sacrifice to Yahweh if sacrifice is an attempt to wrap unrepented sin in a cloak of religious respectability.

> I hate, I despise your feasts,
> and I will not smell [RSV 'I take no delight'] in your solemn assemblies...
> But let justice roll down like waters,
> and righteousness like an everflowing stream. (Amos 5: 21)

However, that is not because God the Father fails to notice them, but because the living God of righteousness chooses not to accept the sacrifices of the unrighteous or to make them efficacious. As Deuteronomy 4: 28 warns the Israelites,

> And there [i.e. in the land of exile where God will have driven them in judgement if they disobey his commands] you will serve gods of wood and stone, the work of men's hands, that neither see, nor hear, nor eat, nor smell.

In other words, they will get no help from that quarter. If, however, they turn back to Yahweh, they will find him a God who acts, a God who remembers his people, hears them and responds to their call in mercy.

> ... for the LORD your God is a merciful God; he will not fail you or destroy you or forget the covenant with your fathers which he swore to them. (v. 31)

Psalm 115 says further of the gods that *'they have feet, but do not walk'*. Mention of Yahweh's 'feet' in the Old Testament usually stresses two of his attributes, his power or his mobility.

> His way is in the whirlwind and storm,
> and the clouds are the dust of his feet. (Nah. 1: 3)

That is one of a number of passages which clearly echo the Canaanite literature in which Ba'al is called 'the Rider of the Clouds'. Such passages have often been called 'Divine Warrior Hymns' (a literary form discussed in the chapter on 'God as Warrior' below). The Canaanite parallels of such a literary form are even clearer in some other passages which celebrate the swift progress of Yahweh, the Warrior, to the help of his people.

> He parted the heavens, and came down,
> thick darkness was under his feet.
> He rode on a cherub, and flew,
> he came swiftly upon the wings of the wind. (Ps. 18: 9-10)

Or again, in Psalm 68, with its clear echo of the Song of Deborah in Judges chapter 5:

> O God, when thou didst go forth before thy people,
> when thou didst march through the wilderness,
> the earth quaked, the heavens poured down rain,
> at the presence of God. (vv. 7-8)

More often, however, God is pictured sitting on his throne with his feet resting on a footstool as monarchs and gods are so often pictured in Ancient Near Eastern iconography. So, to go to the temple, is to go to the place where he sits enthroned in sovereign power over the earth:

> Let us go to his dwelling place,
> let us worship at his footstool. (Ps. 132: 7)

This is in reference to bringing up the 'Ark of the Covenant' to the temple in Jerusalem; other references suggest the ark was seen less as a footstool than as the divine throne itself (e.g. Jer. 3: 16f.), or perhaps as a kind of support for it. In Ezekiel 43: 7, the temple is described by God as 'the place of my throne, and the place of the soles of my feet . . .', and in Isaiah 60: 13 the promise of a restored sanctuary is worded: 'I will make the place of my feet glorious'.

We find then, that the most 'human' talk of God, actually assigning him physical organs of the human body, serves the purpose of exalting his greatness and his 'otherness' rather than bringing him down to human level. It is, of course, boldly anthropomorphic. Yet it seems that there were those who saw clearly that such metaphorical language about God must not be confused with a merely literal sense. In their understanding, God could not be corporeal, a being of flesh and blood. Nowhere is the contrast made more forcefully than by Isaiah when he pours scorn on attempts to find a military ally in Egypt.

> The Egyptians are men, and not God;
> and their horses are flesh, and not spirit. (Isa. 31: 3)

Second Isaiah also stresses the transcendence of God:

> To whom then will you liken me and make me equal,
> and compare me, that we may be alike? (Isa. 46: 5)

* * *

Nevertheless, in spite of careful qualifications, the ascription to God of human organs such as eyes, ears, hands and feet, does not exhaust the ways of speaking of him in human terms. Human emotions and feelings are also ascribed to him. For example, God can 'hate'. We have seen that Amos says this is his feeling towards the religious assemblies and festivals in the sanctuaries of northern Israel. He gets angry. When Moses protested his inability to fulfil the role to which God summoned him with that most understandable of human reactions to the demands of the divine will, 'Oh, my LORD, send, I pray, some other person' (Exod. 4: 13), then we read 'the anger of the LORD was kindled against Moses . . . ' (v. 14).

Extraordinarily, God is said to change his mind. Even the verb 'repent' is used of him. So Amos, glimpsing God's purpose to judge Israel, prays,

> O Lord GOD, forgive, I beseech thee!
> How can Jacob stand?
> He is so small. (Amos 7: 2)

And God's response is described:

> The LORD repented concerning this;
> 'It shall not be,' said the LORD. (v. 3)

Twice that is repeated following the first two of the five visions the prophet sees, but, after them, he does not intercede any more. Perhaps this reflects his realisation that the sins of the nation have become so great that intercession will no longer avail. This would be rather like Jeremiah who was forbidden by God to pray for his people:

> The LORD said to me: 'Do not pray for the welfare of this people. Though they fast, I will not hear their cry . . . .' (Jer. 14: 11)

A little later, the rejection is even more emphatic, though in itself apparently implying that prayer can affect God's purpose:

> Then the LORD said to me, 'Though Moses and Samuel stood before me, yet my heart would not turn toward this people.' (15: 1)

We shall have occasion to speak of God as 'Lover' in a later chapter, but it is surprising how far the attributing of human states of mind to God can go. Indeed, at times, he appears to be subject to some of the limitations of humanity. He does not always appear to be omniscient. For example, the prophet Micaiah has a vision in which he is admitted to the 'Council of Heaven' (one test of the true prophet according to Jer. 23: 18). There he sees God surrounded by his angelic messengers. The occasion is the intention of King Ahaz of Israel and Jehoshaphat, king of Judah, to go to battle against the Syrians at Ramoth-gilead. The four hundred 'court prophets' under Zedekiah have already given an oracle favourable to the enterprise. Micaiah, however, has a very different interpretation of their prophecy. He sees something very much like a Parochial Church Council Meeting in progress, with God in the chair taking counsel from the other members of the committee:

> I saw the LORD sitting on his throne, and all the host of heaven standing beside him on his right hand and on his left; and the LORD said, 'Who will entice Ahab, that he may go up and fall at Ramoth-gilead?' And one said one thing, and another said another. Then a spirit came forward and stood before the LORD, saying, 'I will entice him.' And the LORD said to him, 'By what means?' And he said, 'I will go forth, and will be a lying spirit in the mouth of all his prophets.' And he said, 'You are to entice him, and you shall succeed; go forth and do so.' (I Ki. 22: 19-22).

That appears to be a rather more democratic occasion than we would normally associate with the God of the Old Testament. The members of the committee help the chairman to make up his mind by giving him information he does not have! Again, although this may be due to the dramatic needs of the story, in the Book of Job, God has to ask 'the Satan' where he has been (the Hebrew word means 'adversary' and in Job as in Zechariah 3: 1ff. 'the Satan' appears as a kind of counsel for the prosecution within the Council of Heaven): 'The LORD said to Satan, "Whence have you come?"' (Jb. 1: 6).

Along with this surprising 'humanity' of God goes his capacity for being hurt and for suffering. So Jeremiah portrays God as asking his people:

> What wrong did your fathers find in me
> that they went far from me? (Jer. 2: 5)

This God can only plead with his children, he cannot force them:

> Return, faithless Israel, says the LORD.
> I will not look on you in anger,
> for I am merciful, says the LORD. (Jer. 3: 11)

No one expresses this 'divine weakness' more poignantly than Hosea. God's intentions of love are being constantly thwarted by his people's sin.

> When I would restore the fortunes of my people,
> when I would help Israel,
> the corruption of Ephraim is revealed . . . . (Hos. 7: 1)

God, like a father, had lavished love on the nation in its infancy, but:

> The more I called them,
> the more they went from me. (11: 2)

This leads to the portrayal of an even more remarkable human trait in God, indecision. It is an indecision induced by a conflict of emotions within himself. Their sin, shown by their constant refusal of his love, arouses in him the determination to punish them (vv. 5-7). But this is followed by a confession by God of the torn loyalties and emotions within him, as though the divine justice and the divine love were in conflict and were tearing the divine parent apart.

> How can I give you up, O Ephraim?
> How can I hand you over, O Israel? . . .
> My heart recoils within me,
> my compassion grows warm and tender.
> I will not execute my fierce anger,
> I will not again destroy Ephraim. (vv. 8a, 9)

It is true that those sentences could be read as statements and not as rhetorical questions and so might be interpreted, 'See how I can give you up . . . !' But v. 9 leaves us in little doubt as to which sense is intended. However metaphorical these pictures of inner conflict and indecision within God might be, we cannot escape from the *reality* of the pain and agony within God to which they refer. Here, almost like the 'servant of God' in Isaiah 53, God himself suffers the sin of his people within himself in his love which will not let them go. Indeed, Second Isaiah not only gives us the picture of the 'Suffering Servant' who, in the strength of his weakness redeems others by suffering their sin vicariously; he actually suggests that *God* himself shows some of the characteristics of that servant. God, pleading with his people, says,

> I have not burdened you with offerings,
> or wearied you with frankincense. (Isa. 43: 23b)

The verb translated 'burdened' is related to the noun 'servant' and might be translated, 'I did not put you under bondage' or 'I did not make you serve me over the matter of sacrifices'. Yet, just a little later, the same verbs are used to show what the people have done to God:

> But you have burdened me with your sins,
> you have wearied me with your iniquities. (v. 24b)

So God has been a 'servant' to them by bearing the weight of their sins towards him. Something similar is also the case with Hosea. For Hosea some of the 'conflict' within God himself is eased by God's intention of judging his people as he sends them back from the land he had given them into the wilderness. There Israel, as his faithless 'bride' will be refined and redeemed so that he can bring her back into the land to start all over again. Aptly, the NEB rendering of Hosea 2: 14-16 opens a remarkable insight into God's action in this whole process. It reads:

> I will woo her, I will go with her into the wilderness, and comfort her.

Strictly speaking, the Hebrew verb of the second clause can be rendered simply as, 'I will *cause* her to go into the wilderness.' If, however, God is to 'woo' her and 'comfort' her (Heb. 'speak to her heart'), then presumably he has to be out there *with* his people. So we encounter the thought of the God who judges sin, but who enters himself into that judgement with his people in love, in order to make it a redemptive experience.

Nor is such thought of the 'divine weakness' which proves 'strong' in redemption peculiar only to Hosea and Second Isaiah. God is the God who so loves his people that he bears their sufferings with them. This certainly is the thought expressed in Isaiah 63: 7-9:

> I will recount the steadfast love of the LORD,
> the praises of the LORD,
> according to all that the LORD has granted us,
> and the great goodness to the house of Israel
> which he has granted them according to his mercy,
> according to the abundance of his steadfast love.
> For he said, 'Surely they are my people,
> sons who will not deal falsely;'
> and he became their Saviour.
> In all their affliction he was afflicted,
> and the angel of his presence saved them;
> in his love and in his pity he redeemed them;
> he lifted them up and carried them all the days of old.

This is no impassible God, serene and untroubled upon a throne far removed from the human scene. He takes upon himself his people's suffering. The final phrase 'he lifted them up and carried them all the days of old' is reminiscent of Second Isaiah:

> Even to your old age I am He,
> and to gray hairs I will carry you.
> I have made, and I will bear;
> I will carry and will save. (Isa. 46: 4)

These pictures of God as 'human' in the Old Testament thus take us in two directions. One draws us upwards towards the sovereign God upon his throne. He reigns and presides over all human affairs with power and effectiveness. Yet, even so, this transcendent God wears a human face. When Ezekiel in Babylon had his vision of God coming to him in Babylon on the chariot-throne, amidst all the flashing of lightening and roar of thunder, traditional manifestations of the theophany, he sees that

> ... above the firmament over their heads there was the likeness of a throne, in appearance like sapphire; and seated above the likeness of a throne there was a likeness as it were of a human form.

There in highest heaven is one who, for all the mystery of his glory, can be described as having 'the likeness as it were of a human form'. Significantly, he is surrounded by the appearance of the rainbow, the sign once for all to Noah and to all humankind after him, of his grace and mercy.

The other direction in which these human attributes take us is to the 'weakness' of a God who knows human emotions of love, hate, anger, pity, and who is open to all that is truly human. He knows the hurt, the suffering, the frustration to which love makes the human heart vulnerable. He is at once the supreme, transcendent God, who nevertheless bears humanity in himself into the highest heaven. Yet it is this same God who incarnates himself in all the vicissitudes and sufferings to which humanity is heir. It is in this conjunction in God of divine power and human weakness that hope for the salvation of humanity lies. The New Testament is not entirely unprepared for in the Old.

V

GOD AS KING

Many countries today do not know Monarchy. Even those who do usually have monarchies which have long lost real executive power. This alone would mean that the Old Testament picture of God as 'King' is one of those which needs a great deal of cleaning and restoration work before we can appreciate it. Yet the position is even more complicated, since all the traditions suggest that the institution of monarchy came late into Israel and, regarded as a foreign innovation, it was viewed very differently in the various traditions. Not only, then, do we have to work at getting back to understanding how monarchy was regarded in the Ancient Near East, but we have to be alert to differing views of it in the Old Testament itself and hence to various ways in which the idea of God as 'King' was understood.

To grasp some of these it is necessary to ask first how divine kingship was thought of among Israel's neighbours and what the relationship of the king to the gods was held to be. Then we shall have to examine the various accounts of the rise of monarchy in Israel and the different assessments we find in the Old Testament of its nature and character. Only then shall we be in any position to understand what it meant to a writer of the Old Testament to describe God as 'King'.

Many of Israel's neighbours found the idea of kingship illuminated their understanding of the gods. As with the picture of 'God as Father' this is a picture which is displayed prominently in the literature of the Ancient Near East.[1] In an Egyptian account of the creation of the world the god Re says:

> 'I am Re in his appearances, when he began to rule that which he had made.'

The account goes on to expound this:

> Who is he? This 'Re, when he began to rule that which he had made' means that Re began to appear as a king, as one who was before the liftings of Shu had taken place, when he was on the hill which is in Hermopolis.

The reference to Shu is to an air god who was believed to have lifted heaven from earth. While this is in no way a monotheistic account of creation, Re's kingship is firmly linked with his primal action in creation and is associated with an ancient city, a well-known site for worship. Such places were often described as being on a hill, making them, from the time of creation, places of importance from which the god 'reigned' over their territory. Another text, praising Thebes, speaks similarly of that city:

> Thebes is normal beyond every other city [i.e. she is the standard or 'norm' by which all other cities are to be judged]. The water and land were in her from the first times. Then sand came to delimit the fields and to create her ground on the *hillock*; thus earth came into being.

Another text makes the same claim for Elephantine, a town on the Nile at the southern border of Egypt (where the Aswan Dam is now situated).

> There is a city in the midst of the waters from which the Nile rises named Elephantine . . . It is the . . . primal *hillock* of earth, the *throne* of Re.

Another text dating from the 14th.-12th. centuries BCE describes Re as king, but describes rebellion against him in the same terms as one would describe the insurrection of subjects against a monarch:

> It happened that when Re, the god who came into being by himself, was king of men and gods altogether, mankind plotted something in the presence of Re . . .

GOD AS KING

The text, which is incomplete, goes on to tell how Re takes counsel with other gods and launches action aimed at reasserting his sovereignty over men by a judgement designed to reduce their numbers.

Elsewhere the kingship of Re inspires the devotion of the poet:

> Hail to thee, Amon-Re,
> Lord of the Thrones of the Two Lands,
> Presiding over Karnak . . .
> Lord of what is, who created the fruit tree,
> Made herbage, and gave life to cattle . . .
> The King of Upper and Lower Egypt: Re the triumphant . . .
> The chief one, who made the entire earth.

Here, the idea of Re's kingship is linked with the creation of the world and all the life earth sustains. It is linked further, however, with power and victory. It was only strong Pharaohs who could unite the 'two lands' of Upper and Lower Egypt, and, when they were united, their citizens usually knew peace and order at home and power and influence abroad. The power of the 'divine king', it was felt, must be similarly effective.

In the Egyptian literature, then, the kingship of the gods is linked with creation and with victory through conflict, with consequent order and stability in the realm. For all its world-wide sweep, it is often associated with the idea of the god's presence in a particular city, an important centre of worship, set on a hill from the time of creation. This hilltop setting symbolised its supremacy over a wide region. It is, virtually, the 'centre' of the earth from which the god who is worshipped exercises his world-wide reign.

It is in no way surprising that the Egyptians should have coined the terminology of kingship in their religious vocabulary. Not only does Egyptian civilisation seem to have been centred in monarchy from very early times, but the king was himself seen to be divine, a manifestation of god on earth. The veil separating Pharaoh in his palace from the god on his heavenly throne was a thin one. This could be conceptualised by calling the king the '*Son* of Re'. A king could also be described as 'Horus, Mighty Bull, Appearing in Thebes . . .' (all these being divine appellations used of Thutmose III in annals carved on the walls of the temple in Karnak).

However, some of the most striking testimony describing gods in terms of kingship comes from Mesopotamia. In the Babylonian Epic *Enuma Elish*, a title formed from its opening words meaning 'When on high . . .', we read of the situation before creation:

> When on high the heavens had not been named,
> Firm ground below had not been called by name,
> Naught but primordial Apsu, their begetter,
> And Mummu-Tiamat, she who bore them all,
> Their waters commingling in a single body . . .

Thus, before their ordering in creation, all was a watery chaos, presided over by a dragon monster, Tiamat. Marduk offers to be champion of the gods and engages Tiamat in battle, slaying her and casting the parts of her body to form a 'firmament' to keep the waters of chaos from the earth. He then created the stars and other heavenly bodies and man on the earth to serve the gods. By this great victory Marduk was recognised as king of the gods whom he appointed to their role as guardians in heaven and on earth. The gods build a temple for Marduk in Babylon, the city from which Marduk is believed to reign. Anshar, his father, says:

> Most exalted be the Son, our avenger,
> Let his sovereignty be surpassing, having no rival.

In a later (3rd-2nd. century BCE) Babylonian text we find recorded part of a New Year Festival celebrated in the Spring in which the king of Babylon played a central role. At one point he entered the temple, was divested of his royal insignia and struck on the cheek by the high priest until tears appeared. He knelt to protest his innocence and faithful obedience to the laws of the gods in his reign and only then was re-admitted to royal honour. It is not clear whether this was seen as a re-enactment of Marduk's battle with the forces of chaos, but certainly that victory of Marduk was celebrated and his divine kingship acclaimed. The priest addressed Bel, a title for Marduk, the State god of Babylon:

> Lord of the world, king of the gods, divine Marduk,
> who establishes the plan,
> Important, elevated, exalted, supreme,
> who holds kingship, grasps lordship.

So Marduk's kingship is clearly associated with his act of creation, an act accomplished through conflict with the forces of chaos. It is this which makes possible the yearly cycle of the seasons with their periods of rain, making the soil fertile. The purpose of the Babylonian New Year Festival was to purify the temple and ensure that the king on earth was reigning with justice and compassion. So Marduk's kingship produces a just social order in the community as well as ensuring prosperity based on a fertile soil. Again, as in the Egyptian texts, Marduk's reign is linked with a city, in this case Babylon. For all the lateness of the text just cited, there is no reason to doubt that it enshrined older beliefs and practices.

Nearer to Israel were the Canaanites, whose land Israel gradually took over and whose influence, as they were absorbed into the Israelite monarchic kingdom, was strong on Israel's life and religion. Their literature also testifies to a version of this myth of a primeval conflict. In their case the god is Ba'al who fought the sea-god Yam (the Hebrew word for 'sea'). We read their version of it in the Epic poem *Ba'al* from the Ugaritic texts.[2] After an initial setback at Yam's hands, Ba'al is encouraged by Kothar-and-Hasis (the divine craftsman who is later to build a temple for Ba'al) who puts two clubs into Ba'al's hands with which he strikes Yam. Both are needed for only the second deals the *coup-de-grâce*:

> The mace whirled in Ba'al's hands
> Like an eagle in his fingers
> crushed the pate of Prince Yam
> the forehead of judge Nahar (= 'River').
> Yam collapsed and fell down to the earth,
> his face quivered and his features crumpled up.

It appears that Ba'al also scattered Yam's broken body as Marduk scattered Tiamat's. Following the victory, Ashtarte, the goddess, cries out in triumph, 'Verily Yam is dead! Ba'al shall be king'.

Later texts tell of a palace-temple built for Ba'al just as one had been built for Marduk at Babylon. There are many problems posed by the texts, partly because they are incomplete and partly because it is difficult to relate them to each other. Others tell of conflict with the god *Môth* (= 'Death'), of a great monster, *Lotan*, (= Leviathan in the Old Testament, e.g. Isa. 27: 1). The conflict with Yam is not linked explicitly with creation, although in other texts the conflicts with *Môth* and *Lotan* clearly are. For our purpose here, however, it is enough to observe that Ba'al is seen as king as a result of the victory he achieves in combat and that, again, his rule is associated with a temple-palace.

To summarise this section of our study we can say that the concept of the gods in terms of 'kingship' was widespread among Israel's neighbours. In general it is understood in terms of creation and order in the universe by virtue of the god's power to subdue those forces of chaos and infertility which threaten to disrupt the kingdom, and sometimes it is seen as a guarantee of moral order and justice in the world of human society. So the Babylonian sun god *Shamash* (*shemesh* being the Hebrew word for 'sun') is addressed in one royal inscription:

> To Shamash, the *king* of heaven and earth, the magistrate of gods and man.

He was in fact the Judge in the Babylonian pantheon. So it is not surprising to find the great Babylonian king, Hammurabi, (c. 1792-1750 BCE) stating in the law code which was drawn up in his reign,

> By the order of Shamash, the great judge of heaven
> and earth, may my justice prevail in the land.

Power to achieve victory enables a king to enforce justice. Power and justice are two vital aspects of kingship in the ancient world. It is not surprising that, when people saw the power of the forces of creation, and the order of nature, with its ever-recurring seasons, and when they longed for a moral order of justice and truth in their human society, they should think longingly of their gods as the ultimate and final embodiment of ideal kingship. Human kings, ideally, brought about a projection

GOD AS KING

on earth of the rule of the god. It was only by the help of the gods that these human kings could faithfully represent their ideal counterparts in heaven. Divine kingship was the ultimate source of hope for peace and righteousness on earth. Equally, it was the divine king who sanctioned the government of his representative king on earth. It was thus the god who gave validity both to the claims of the king to rule and to the city where he reigned as the properly designated place where the god and his vice-gerent should dwell.

・・・・・・・・・・・・・・・・・・・・

It may seem to have been natural for areas such as Egypt, Mesopotamia and even Canaan to have pictured their gods as 'kings'. All seem to have known kingship from an early time, if not nationally, then in individual city states. At first glance, however, it is more surprising that Israel should have adopted it as a picture of their God, Yahweh, and to have made such extensive religious use of it in their sacred writings. All traditions seem to agree that kingship was not original to Israelite society and there are mixed views in the Old Testament as to its value.

These different views become apparent in the accounts of the origins of kingship. Even a superficial reading of the texts of I Samuel 8: 1-22 and I Samuel 9: 1-27 reveals two distinct accounts of the installation of Saul as king by Samuel, and two very different evaluations of the rightness or wrongness of the action. The account in I Samuel 9: 1-27 tells how Saul went with his servant to look for his father's lost asses. At the servant's suggestion they turn aside to consult Samuel who figures in this story as a local 'holy man', unknown to Saul, who, on payment of a fee, might be induced to reveal the whereabouts of the herd by an act of divination. The point of view of the story is strongly pro-monarchic and strongly pro-Saul, as opposed to later traditions which tended to favour David over against Saul. God has already revealed Saul's coming visit to Samuel:

> 'Tomorrow about this time I will send to you a man from the land of Benjamin, and you shall anoint him to be prince over my people Israel. He shall save my people from the hand of the

Philistines; for I have seen the affliction of my people, because their cry has come to me.' (I Sam. 9: 16)

Here, monarchy is God's idea, of his devising and appointing. It is his chosen instrument for the salvation of his people. In I Samuel 8, however, monarchy is seen to be the result of *rebellion* by the Israelites against the rule of God and even, in some measure, against the role of the prophet as mediator in the divine rule of God over his people. They act from the suspect motive (according to the narrator) of a desire to be 'like the other nations' (v. 4), a thing which the Deuteronomists[3] saw as a denial of Israel's call to be a people separated from the nations as God's 'inheritance' (e.g. Deut. 4: 15-20). God is represented as grudgingly permitting his prophet to accede to their request:

> And the LORD said to Samuel, 'Hearken to the voice of the people in all that they say to you; for they have not rejected you, but they have rejected me from being king over them.' (I Sam. 8: 7)

However he is to warn them of the tyrannical nature of monarchy and this he does with a relish and thoroughness which could provide a charter for republicans down the ages (vv. 10-18).

Both these views of monarchy find voice elsewhere in the Old Testament. The favourable view of I Samuel 9 is found in Judges 17: 6, 21: 25, verses which look back on pre-monarchic days as times of anarchy :

> In those days there was no king in Israel; every man did what was right in his own eyes.

A positive view also occurs in the so-called 'Last Words of David' in II Samuel 23: 1-7, a speech described as the oracle of David, 'the man who was raised on high, the anointed of the God of Jacob' (v. 1). This expresses the faith that

> When one rules justly over men,
> ruling in the fear of God,
> he dawns on them like the morning light . . . (vv. 3b, 4a)

II Samuel chapter 7 might be called the 'foundation charter' of the pro-monarchic view. It is not only pro-monarchic in general, but pro-*dynastic* monarchy and pro-*Davidic* dynastic monarchy in particular. In rejecting David's wish to build a temple ('house') for God, Nathan the prophet brings him the assurance,

> 'Moreover the LORD declares to you that the LORD will make you a house . . . And your house and your kingdom shall be made sure before me; your throne shall be established for ever.' (vv. 11b, 16)

The triumph of the 'dynastic' view of monarchy (i.e. a ruling line where the oldest son always succeeds to the throne) over the 'charismatic' view of kingship (i.e. where prophet and people make someone king on recognition of some outstanding quality in him) puts much greater centralised power in its hands. Consent of prophets and assembly become dispensable. The triumph of this view is represented in many Psalms, especially the so-called 'royal' Psalms. These almost certainly formed part of the liturgy of the worship in the temple in Jerusalem which, from the time of Solomon onwards, became a 'royal chapel' serving the interests of a Yahwism which had become a 'State' religion. So the king is seen as God's 'son' (Ps. 2: 7), God's 'anointed' (the Hebrew for this gives us the word '*Messiah*', v. 2), a priest-king leading in the service of the royal cult of Yahwism (Ps. 110: 4) assured always of God's victory over his enemies (vv. 1, 2, 5f.). The everlasting continuance of the Davidic line is affirmed by the most solemn divine oaths:

> Once for all I have sworn by my holiness;
> I will not lie to David.
> His line shall endure for ever. (Ps. 89: 35-36)

This king is the safeguard of moral order and justice in society (Ps. 72: 1-4), God's vice-gerent on earth. While foreign influence on all this, especially that of Egypt, seems likely in view of what we learned about monarchy among Israel's neighbours, nowhere do these Psalms go as far as to suggest that the king is 'divine'. The need for his dependence upon and obedience to God are often stressed (e.g. Ps. 132: 12). Nevertheless that same Psalm links the divine choice of the Davidic line and of the city of Jerusalem as his dwelling place 'for ever' (v. 14) in a way which makes Yahwism very much the buttress and sanction for the Davidic monarchy. It reminds us of the ancient idea of the rule of a god being exercised through a human regent in a city raised on a hill (Ps. 48: 1f.).

Elsewhere in the Old Testament, however, very different views of monarchy are to be found. Gideon is apparently offered kingship by those described as 'the men of Israel' (Ju. 8:22), although probably it was an offer local to the area of Shechem, rather than to Israel as a whole. There are several obscurities in the incident. The noun 'King' is not used nor the verb which derives from it meaning 'to rule as king'. Nevertheless, the nature of Gideon's reply seems to suggest that it was to a dynastic monarchy that he had been summoned:

> Gideon said to them, 'I will not rule over you, and my son will not rule over you; the LORD will rule over you.' (v. 23)

It is not impossible that this is a later editorial comment since the the rest of the chapter, with its account of Gideon exacting tribute to make an ephod which he put in *'his* city' (v. 27), as well as his leading them to victory against the Midianites, might suggest that, in the original narrative, he accepted the offer.[4] However, the point of view of v. 22 agrees with the anti-monarchic view of I Samuel 8:7 which sees appointment of a man as king as an infringement of Yahweh's kingship over his people.

Jotham's fable (Ju. 9: 7-15) is a scathing indictment of the institution of monarchy. The trees decided to appoint one of their number to be king over them. They approached first the olive and then the fig tree, but both these valuable trees scorned the idea of abandoning their useful role to act as anything as worthless as a king. So in desperation the trees turn to the bramble. Only something as useless as that could be persuaded to accept. In context, the fable is directed against the rule of Abimelech, but it is clear that originally it must have been anti-monarchic as such, for it does not really fit its present context. The sons of Jerubba'al had not *refused* the kingship, but had been supplanted in favour of Abimelech.

Hosea is also scathing about the institution. Speaking of the evil committed and tolerated in the society of eighth century northern Israel he says:

> By their wickedness they make the king glad,
> and the princes by their treachery. (7: 3)

Again, threatening God's judgement which will take the form of invasion by powerful enemies, he asks in scorn:

> Where is now your king, to save you:
> where are all your princes to defend you –
> those of whom you said,
> 'Give me a king and princes?'
> I have given you kings in my anger
> and I have taken them away in my wrath. (13: 11)

It is a nice point whether Hosea rejected kingship as such, or was passing adverse comment on particular northern kings, much as the editors of the Books of Kings (the 'Deuteronomistic' editors as they are often called, see ch. 2, n. 2) pass sentence on each individual king as to whether he did what was 'right' in the eyes of Yahweh or, much more often, what was 'wrong' in his eyes.[5] The result is the same, a rejection of monarchy as it was known in the later years of the life of the northern kingdom.

Another passage which expresses a view of monarchy markedly different from the eulogies of the royal psalms is Deuteronomy 17: 14-20. This allows for monarchy, but hedges it about with some very pointed limitations:

> When you come to the land . . . and then say, 'I will set a king over me, like all the nations that are round about me'; you may indeed set as king over you him whom the LORD your God will choose . . . Only he must not multiply horses for himself [i.e. a sign of trust in human military might] . . . and he shall not multiply wives for himself, lest his heart turn away; nor shall he greatly multiply for himself silver and gold. And when he sits on the throne of his kingdom, he shall write for himself in a book a copy of this law . . . and he shall read in it all the days of his life . . . that his heart may not be lifted up above his brethren. (17: 14-19)

Solomon please note! It is difficult to see this as other than a warning against what the monarchy became under Solomon.[6] It seems to be an attempt to stem what was seen by some as a tendency towards the greater centralisation of power and 'absolutism' of monarchy.

It should also be noted that three strategic passages in the 'Deuteronomistic History' qualify the 'unconditional' nature of the promise made by God to David through Nathan that his line would last for ever. They introduce a conditional note. When David is dying he instructs his son, Solomon, to keep carefully the laws of God 'that the LORD may establish his word which he spoke concerning me saying, *"If your sons take heed to their way . . .* there shall not fail you a man to sit on the throne of Israel."' (I Ki. 2: 4, cf. I Ki. 8: 25, 9: 4f.)

Finally, we should note that in some later 'eschatological' prophecy, no restoration of the monarchy is envisaged. Second Isaiah, for example, does not mention a renewal of the Davidic monarchy after the return from Babylon. Instead, he seems to see a kind of 'democratisation' of it by which the whole community inherits the special place of David (Isa. 55: 3-5), while Ezekiel 40-48 pointedly does not give the leader the old Hebrew name for 'king' (*melek*).

It is interesting to ask, at this point, why the editors of the history books allowed two such contrasting estimates of the rise of the monarchy to stand side by side in I Samuel chapters 8 and 9. It may well be to make a very sophisticated theological point. Perhaps they were saying that the monarchy, like any human institution, is ambivalent. Used aright, in obedience to God's laws and in concern for the well-being of its subjects and justice in society, it can be an instrument for good. Abused, it can all too easily become an instrument of tyranny and corruption. One cannot say that one of these accounts was 'right' and the other 'wrong'. Later Israelite kings illustrated the truth of both of them.

In the face of this divided view of monarchy in the Old Testament then, it may seem surprising that it still furnished a model for talk about God. In fact, the division of view may not have made all that difference because *both* factions had different, but equally valid reasons, for using it. On the one hand the protagonists for monarchy could see in human monarchy a valid model for understanding the kingship of God. Among these supporters the most significant group, as we have seen, were involved in the royal worship of the temple in Jerusalem as represented by many Psalms, but they also included those prophets, like Isaiah, who owed something to its influence. On the other hand, those who became disillusioned with human kingship also had good reason to speak of God as King, for in their eyes he alone was the guardian of the true values of kingship.

It is impossible now to know when the idea of God as King began in Israel. The 'anti-monarchic' sources we have mentioned see monarchy as usurping an earlier kingship of God himself over Israel, and other passages have been pressed into service to argue for this early understanding in Israel.[7] We do not know the date of these passages, however. Some argue that the idea of God as the true King would only have been intelligible once monarchy had been adopted; but on this point, others argue that there had always been the example of neighbouring countries to provide the picture. They say that the Hebrew word for 'King' (*melek*) and its related verb had an earlier meaning of 'to guide' or 'to lead'.[8] In fact, any attempt to chart some alleged historical development of the concept would be as hazardous with this picture of God as with any other.

....

When we considered the Old Testament picture of God as 'Father' we looked first to see what the Israelites understood by 'fatherhood'. We must do the same with the picture of God as 'King', for all the different responses the institution aroused. Perhaps the clearest expression of the expectations aroused is heard in, of all places, the 'anti-monarchic' source in I Samuel 8. In v. 20 the people are reported to have exclaimed:

> No! but we will have a king over us . . . that our king may govern us [the Hebrew verb means 'judge us'] and go out before us and fight our battles.

These two facets of monarchy, the execution of justice and the role of military leader, were seen as obverse and reverse of the same thing. Ideally, at least, the king was the ultimate embodiment of justice, but, as we have seen to be the case with monarchy among Israel's neighbours, to administer justice he had to have power over all dissident elements in his own realm and be able to fight off the intrusions of others from outside. These, if they gained control of the realm, could deny its citizens their 'justice'. As one writer has said, '. . . one of the essentials of any legal system is the ability to enforce legal decisions . . . .'[9]

Just how important this concept was to Israel is seen in the prayer with which Psalm 72 opens:

> Give the king thy justice, O God,
> and thy righteousness to the royal son!
> May he judge thy people with righteousness
> and thy poor with justice.

When we recall how often the prophets had to attack the wealthy and powerful for their oppression of the poor, we can understand how vital it was that the king should be a just and true champion of their cause, administering justice impartially, without fear or favour or 'bending' the rules for those who could and would pay the necessary bribe. So the Psalmist shows later that the truly just king

> delivers the needy when he calls,
> the poor and him who has no helper.
> He has pity on the weak and needy,
> and saves the lives of the needy.
> From oppression and violence he redeems their life;
> and precious is their blood in his sight. (vv. 12-14)

To achieve this, however, he must have the power to rule in his realm, and so the Psalm includes a prayer for his victory in battle:

> May he have dominion from sea to sea,
> and from the River to the ends of the earth!
> May his foes bow down before him,
> and his enemies lick the dust! (vv. 8f.)

When the king ruled thus powerfully and justly he was protecting his realm from the power of chaos, and so the whole land would know peace and prosperity (v. 7). Indeed, the nation would so know the blessing of God that the land itself would become fertile:

> May there be abundance of grain in the land;
> on the tops of the mountains may it wave. (v. 16)

All traditions assert that monarchy began in a time of military crisis and both Saul and David were anointed king because of their prowess in battle. But tradition in the Old Testament also shows how firmly the king was associated with the administration of justice in the realm. The famous story of Solomon and the two prostitutes, with his canny verdict which showed who was the true mother of the baby, is an example of this (I Ki. 3: 16-27). It was evidently the practice for anyone in the realm to be able to come to the king as a final court of appeal (although it is unlikely, especially in later times, that the king would have seen all supplicants personally). Perhaps the story of Moses appointing administrative assistants (Exod. 18: 15-26) gives an indication of what happened in later, monarchical times. Certainly, Absalom was able to make use of the people's discontent with David's failure to hear all their cases (II Sam. 15: 1-6). Again, in the tradition, both Jehoshaphat (II Chr. 19: 4-11) and Josiah (II Ki. chs. 22f.) are associated with legal reforms. So Proverbs can make one of the most absolute of statements:

> Inspired decisions are on the lips of a king;
> his mouth does not sin in judgement. (Prov. 16: 10)[10]

No doubt much of all this belongs to the realm of the ideal and comes from court circles whose aim was royal propoganda. There is plenty of evidence that, in practice, the ideal was often missed, or even cynically disregarded. Nevertheless, the ideal tells us what expectations were fastened upon the 'king'. He was the protector and guardian of the nation against its enemies without and its oppressive and tyrannical forces within. He was the final court of appeal who would administer true justice for those who had neither the power nor the wealth to secure a favourable verdict in local courts. He was the one through whom God's rule over the nation was exercised and so he mediated to the people all those blessings of creation which were the result of God's original victory over the forces of chaos. By his right relationship with God he helped to keep those ever-threatening forces of chaos at bay. So through the king the whole society enjoyed *shālôm*. He was the 'life' of the body politic. In exile one writer looked back sadly on the king who was no longer on the throne in Jerusalem and reflected that he was

> The breath of our nostrils, the LORD's anointed . . .
> he of whom we said, 'Under his shadow
> we shall live among the nations.' (Lam. 4: 20)

In another metaphor, David's men are represented as wanting to save him from the dangers of the front line in battle, 'Lest,' they say, 'thou quench the *lamp* of Israel.' (II Sam. 20: 17, cf. I Ki. 11: 36, 15: 4)

The 'light' and the 'life' of the nation—that, ideally, was what kingship meant for the people of Israel.

. . . .

It is Yahweh's *power* which is the foundation on which his throne rests securely and from which he reigns as king effectively. This power was manifested by his act in creation when he, like Marduk and Ba'al, drove back the powers of chaos and defeated the dragon monster. This was a theme prominent in the worship of the Jerusalem temple:

> Yet God my *king* is from of old,
> working salvation in the midst of the earth.
> Thou didst divide the sea by thy might,
> thou didst break the heads of the dragons on the waters.
> Thou didst crush the heads of Leviathan,[11]
> thou didst give him as food for the creatures of the wilderness . . .
> Thine is the day, thine also the night;
> thou hast established the luminaries and the sun.
> Thou hast fixed all the bounds of the earth;
> thou hast made summer and winter. (Ps. 74: 13f., 16f.)

GOD AS KING

It may be that there is a hint in vv. 13f. of the salvation event of the deliverance across the Reed Sea, although the emphasis of the context is on the creation of the world. But it is no coincidence that the two ideas merge into each other. Because God has demonstrated his power at creation in driving back and containing the waters that represent chaos and which threaten always to engulf the world, he, as Saviour, is able to keep them at bay by his continuing acts in the world and its history.

Second Isaiah also recalls the creation victory motif, only to link it at once with God's salvation at the time of the Exodus:

> Awake, awake, put on strength,
> O arm of the LORD . . . .
> Was it not thou that didst cut Rahab in pieces,
> that didst pierce the dragon?
> Was it not thou that didst dry up the sea,
> the waters of the great deep;
> that didst make the depths of the sea a way
> for the redeemed to pass over? (Isa. 51: 9f.)

Indeed, it is important to see that the reference in Psalm 74 to God as king by virtue of his victory in the act of creation is set in the context of a cry to God for help at a moment of need in history. The Psalm appears to belong to the time of the exile or, at least, to some time of national crisis when the enemy is rampaging through Jerusalem and assaulting even God's holy temple:

> Thy foes have roared in the midst of thy holy place;
> they set up their own signs for signs . . .
> They set thy sanctuary on fire;
> to the ground they desecrated the dwelling place of thy name.
> (Ps. 74: 4,7)

Still the Psalmist remembers

> Yet God my King is from of old,
> working salvation in the midst of the earth.' (v. 12)

This becomes the basis of his plea that God will repeat the miracle of his victory over the forces of chaos now, in this particular time:

> Arise, O God, plead thy cause;
> remember how the impious scoff at thee all the day!
> Do not forget the clamour of thy foes,
> the uproar of thy adversaries which goes up continually. (vv. 22f.)

The theme of God's effective kingly rule based on the power by which he can cause his writ to run throughout the realm is the basis both for praise and prayer. Psalm 29 opens with a call to the powers in heaven to pay homage to God:

> Ascribe to the LORD, O heavenly beings,
> ascribe to the LORD glory and strength.
> Ascribe to the LORD the glory of his name;
> worship the LORD in holy array. (vv. 1f.)

The Psalm then continues by recalling God's victory over the forces of watery chaos in creation:

> The voice of the LORD is upon the waters;
> the God of glory thunders,
> the LORD, upon many waters. (v. 3)

This leads up to the triumphant assertion:

> The LORD sits enthroned upon the flood;
> the LORD sits enthroned as king for ever. (v. 10)

The climax of all this is a statement of the consequences for his people. He gives 'strength to his people' (v. 11). He is an effective leader who enables them to face and overcome their 'foes' of every kind. His strong, effective rule results in *shālôm* for his people, which implies not only the absence of civil unrest or active warfare, but all that makes for fullness of life by bringing prosperity, health, order and justice to the community. Indeed, most of the psalms which celebrate God's kingship[12] seem to contain three elements: a) the note of conflict, by which the kingship of God is threatened in some way; b) the affirmation of God's power and rule as king, and c) the consequence of this for his people.

So Psalm 47 calls upon all nature to acknowledge God:

> Clap your hands, all peoples!
> Shout to God with loud songs of joy!
> For the LORD, the Most High, is terrible,
> a great king over all the earth. (vv. 1-2)

Yet this kingship was achieved and demonstrated by his victory in conflict, this time against Israel's historical enemies:

> He subdued peoples under us,
> and nations under our feet. (v. 3)

Such victories resulted in his gift of the land as a 'heritage' for his people:

> He chose our heritage for us,
> the pride of Jacob whom he loves. (v. 4)

In Psalm 93 the victory of Yahweh was over the waters of chaos:

> The floods have lifted up, O LORD,
> the floods have lifted up their voice,
> the floods lift up their roaring.
> Mightier than the thunders of many waters,
> mightier than the waves of the sea,
> the LORD on high is mighty. (vv. 3f)

The consequences of this victory are the order and stability of creation:

> Yea, the world is established;
> it shall never be moved. (v. 1b)

Even more, the utter reliability of Yahweh's decrees may now be trusted, those promises and commandments which bind his covenant people to himself. 'Holiness' is mediated by his presence among them:

> Thy decrees are very sure;
> holiness befits thy house,
> O LORD for evermore. (v. 5)

Psalm 95 sees the 'kingship' of God, shown in his acts of creation, as the basis of the covenant relationship between him and his people. It therefore forms the basis of the call for his covenant people to worship him:

> O come, let us worship and bow down,
> let us kneel before the LORD, our Maker!
> For he is our God,
> and we are the people of his pasture,
> and the sheep of his hand. (vv. 6f.)

But this also means obeying him:

> O that today you would hearken to his voice!
> Harden not your hearts, as at Meribah,
> as on the day at Massah in the wilderness . . . . (vv. 7f, 8)

In Psalm 97 his victory in creation is hymned, since the result of this is that worshippers of false gods are confounded, in contrast to Israel who can rejoice in God and trust him completely because of his absolute power:

> All worshippers of images are put to shame,
> who make their boast in worthless idols;
> all gods bow down before him.
> Zion hears and is glad,
> and the daughters of Judah rejoice,
> because of thy judgements, O God. (vv. 7f.)

Further, moral order reigns in God's kingdom, whereby those who hate evil are protected and prosper:

> The LORD loves those who hate evil;
> he preserves the lives of the saints;
> he delivers them from the hand of the wicked.
> Light dawns for the righteous,
> and joy for the upright in heart. (vv. 10f.)

Similarly, Psalm 98 finds God's victory in creation the basis of a call to all the earth to worship (vv. 4-8), for his rule results in God's righteous judgement of the earth whereby he establishes and promotes the cause of justice and righteousness in the community:

> . . .for he comes to judge the earth.
> He will judge the world with righteousness,
> and the peoples with equity. (v. 9)

It is this same confidence which forms the basis of cries for help in times of danger and distress. It appears as 'the ground of confidence' underlying many of the Psalms of lament.

> Hearken to the sound of my cry,
> my King and my God,
> for to thee do I pray. (Ps. 5: 2)

The Psalmist, whether he is king or commoner, is appealing against the ravages caused by those who 'boast', 'do evil' (vv. 5-6), and distort the truth with falsehood in pursuit of their own ends (vv. 6-7). They subvert the just and peaceful order of society. In effect, they are in rebellion against the rule and authority of God, the King, 'for they have rebelled against thee' (vv. 10-11). The same verdict will be a legal decision in favour of those who are innocent:

> But let all who take refuge in thee rejoice,
> let them ever sing for joy;
> and do thou defend them,
> that those who love thy name may exult in thee.
> For thou dost bless the righteous, O LORD;
> thou dost cover him with favour as with a shield. (vv. 11-12)

Here, the idea of the king's legal power to establish justice in his realm and his military power to protect his people from their enemies are to the fore. The justice and power of God as 'king' are clearly stated in vv. 4-6:

> For thou art not a God who delights in wickedness;
> evil may not sojourn with thee.

> The boastful may not stand before thy eyes;
> thou hatest all evil doers.
> Thou destroyest those who speak lies;
> the LORD abhors bloodthirsty and deceitful men.

In Psalm 10 the kingship of God is again hymned: 'The LORD is king for ever and ever' (v. 16a); so all invading nations will be conquered—'the nations shall perish from his land' (v. 16b). This Psalm is usually held to form a unity with Psalm 9 which also celebrates God's kingship:

> But the LORD sits enthroned for ever.
> he has established his throne for judgement;
> and he judges the world with righteousness,
> he judges the people with equity. (vv. 7-8)

This is theme both for praise and for cry for help from the worshipper who knows persecution from the powerful and apparently successful 'wicked' (10: 1f., 5). Like the 'just king' God will surely intervene:

> O LORD, thou wilt hear the desire of the meek;
> thou wilt strengthen their heart,
> thou wilt incline thine ear
> to do justice to the fatherless and the oppressed,
> so that man who is of earth may strike terror no more. (Ps. 10: 17f.)

God's military power to overcome his foes is the basis of the call in Psalm 44: 4, 'Thou art my King and my God . . .' Surely therefore he will come to the rescue of his people in the time of defeat:

> Rise up, come to our help!
> Deliver us for the sake of thy steadfast love! (vv. 23-24)

The conection of God as King with a particular place, a note we heard in other Ancient Near Eastern literature, is also to be caught in the Psalms:

> Great is the LORD and greatly to be praised
> in the city of our God!
> His holy mountain, beautiful in elevation,
> is the joy of all the earth,
> Mount Zion, in the far north,
> the city of the great King. (Ps. 48: 1-2)

Indeed, there is a clear echo of the Canaanite literature here. Mount 'Zaphon' in the Ba'al epic literature is the abode of the gods, just as Mount Olympus was in Greek mythology. It means 'Mount North', hence the allusion to Zion as 'the city in the far north' in Psalm 48.

This association between God as King and his city Jerusalem can provide the basis of a cry for help uttered in the sanctuary:

> How lovely is thy dwelling place,
> O LORD of hosts!
> My soul longs, yea, faints
> for the courts of the LORD . . .
> Even the sparrow finds a home,
> and the swallow a nest for herself,
> where she may lay her young,
> at thy altars, O LORD of hosts,
> my King and my God. (Ps. 84: 1-3)

So God will hear the cry of the people for their own king, their 'shield' and the 'Messiah' (='anointed one') of Yahweh:

> O LORD God of hosts, hear my prayer
> give ear, O God of Jacob!
> Behold our shield, O God;
> look upon the face of thine anointed! (vv. 8-9)

Indeed, God himself, as heavenly king, is both 'shield' and 'light' to his people, and so may be trusted to give 'grace' and 'honour'. He will not refuse to give any 'good' to his people:

> For the LORD God is a sun and a shield;
> he bestows favour and honour.
> No good thing does the LORD withold
> from those who walk uprightly. (v. 11)

A very interesting expression of the same confidence is found in a prophetic book. In Isaiah chapter 6 the prophet describes his call-vision in the temple:

> In the year that King Uzziah died I saw the Lord sitting upon a *throne*, high and lifted up; and his train filled the temple. (Isa. 6: 1)

He hears the praise of the seraphim, fiery serpents often depicted in ancient near eastern temple art as guarding the approach to the royal or divine presence.

> Holy, holy, holy is the LORD of hosts;
> the whole earth is full of his glory. (v. 3)

This vision of the transcendence of God is thus portrayed in terms of kingship, so that all through the earth there is that which can be seen of his presence, namely, his 'glory'; in the face of this, Isaiah becomes aware that the divine king, who is himself righteous, is a force making for righteousness throughout his realm. This brings a deep sense of his own sin and that of the nation which at this point he represents:

> And I said, 'Woe is me! For I am lost; for I am a man of unclean lips, and I dwell in the midst of a people of unclean lips; for my eyes have seen the King, the LORD of hosts!' (v. 5)

Although the exact origin of the phrase 'LORD of Hosts' is disputed (it will be discussed in our chapter on 'God as Warrior' below), it undoubtedly highlights God's power as king over all. It is significant that Isaiah sees God, the king, as working for righteousness, not only in judgement (vv. 11-13) but in grace, for he himself is cleansed by an act of divine grace (vv. 6f.) It is small wonder that he sees the possibility of that grace making the whole community righteous, even if it has to be the other side of judgement (1: 21-26). For Isaiah, Yahweh's royal power upon his universal throne is so complete that he can see the great military power of his day, Assyria, as nothing more than a tool in God's hands (10: 15) with which to accomplish his work (10: 5f., 12). When this has been done the universal King will punish Assyria itself for its arrogant pride (10: 7-11, 12-19). From his own people the only fit response before the sovereign power of God is complete, dependent trust (7: 9b, 30: 15). This involves turning away from all self-sufficiency (2: 12), from all trust in other human powers (31: 1-3) and from all disobedience to God's ethical demands (5: 7).

Isaiah's portrayal of God as 'king' is an important witness to the prophetic use of this picture, for it is not prominent in all prophetic literature. It is perhaps significant that Isaiah comes from the south and seems to be familiar with the David/Zion traditions. Yet his use of the picture to challenge the people to obedience should make us wary of those who claim that the prophets avoided using it because of its facile associations with the falsely optimistic royal and national hopes of the Jerusalem cultus. For example, Ezekiel's call-vision (Ezek. 1) clearly echoes some aspects of Isaiah 6, except that in Ezekiel's picture the throne on which Yahweh is seated as universal King is mobile, and seen by the prophet in Babylon, far from Jerusalem. The vision is narrated in a form which suggests that Yahweh's writ as universal king runs throughout all the earth, all parts of which are accessible to his sight and his presence, and all subject to his divine control. After describing the living creatures which supported the 'throne-chariot', it continues:

> And above the firmament over their heads there was the likeness of a throne, in appearance like sapphire; and seated above the likeness of a throne was a likeness as it were of a human form ... Such was the appearance of the likeness of the glory of the LORD. (1: 26, 28)

There is no false comfort in Ezekiel's doctrine of the universal kingship of Yahweh for the Jews of Judah and Jerusalem or for those in exile in Babylon. While, ultimately, his sovereign purpose is to renew the nation 'for his name's sake', this will not be before judgement for sin has swept away all false grounds of confidence in their own claims on Yahweh by virtue of the covenant or the zeal of their worship (e.g. 12: 1-16, 33: 23-29).

It is in Second Isaiah, that great prophet of the Babylonian exile who stands most clearly in line with what must be thought of as an Isaianic tradition centred on the Zion theology, that we find God's kingship to be a main theme of joy and praise. Even more, it is the ground of hope for the future salvation for his people. Addressing the gods of the nations in sarcasm, God summons them to trial:

> 'set forth your case,' says the LORD;
> 'bring your proofs,' says the King of Jacob.
> 'Let them bring them, and tell us what is to happen . . .
> Tell us what is to come hereafter,
> that we may know that you are gods.' (Isa. 41: 21, 23)

By contrast, God, by his powerful creative word has declared beforehand through his prophets what he would do. Now he is fulfilling his purpose in the salvation of his people, for such is his lordship over human beings, nations and the events of history:

> I stirred up one from the north,
> and he has come, from the rising of the sun, and he shall call on my name . . .
> I first have declared it to Zion,
> and I give to Jerusalem a herald of good tidings. (41: 25, 27)

It is because God is creator and so lord of the forces of nature and history, that he is able to be the deliverer of his people:

> I am the LORD, your Holy One,
> the Creator of Israel, your King.
> Thus says the LORD,
> who makes a way in the sea,
> a path in the mighty waters . . . . (43: 15f.)

Again the reference is both to Creation and to the events of the Exodus. Nevertheless, what he is about to do in rescuing Israel from captivity in Babylon and bringing them home will eclipse the former events of redemption from Egypt:

> Remember not the former things,
> nor consider the things of old.
> Behold I am doing a new thing . . . . (43: 18f.)

His kingship is shown now in his eclipsing of all those which must be described as 'non-gods':

> Thus says the LORD, the King of Israel
> and his Redeemer, the LORD of hosts:
> 'I am the first and I am the last;
> besides me there is no god.' (44: 6)

This takes up the theme of the kingship of God as it was celebrated in the worship in Zion. There, in the 'Enthronement Psalms', his kingship was proved and asserted by his victory over the false gods and all the forces of chaos. If now in the present the Israelites do not see the peace, order, justice and joy of his reign, all this is shortly to be changed as he acts for their salvation.

No doubt it is this tradition which proved a fertile seed-bed for eschatological hope for the future in later prophecy. So we read:

> And the LORD will become king over all the earth: on that day
> the LORD will be one and his name one. (Zech. 14: 9)

All peoples will unite to acknowledge the sole, universal kingship of the God of Israel:

> The King of Israel, the LORD, is in your midst;
> you shall fear evil no more . . .
> The LORD, your God, is in your midst,
> a warrior who gives victory. (Zeph. 3: 15b, 17a)

A late resurgence of this concept of Yahweh's primeval victory over the forces of chaos and evil as something which will recur at the end-time is found in Daniel chapter 7. Written in the second century BCE against the background of persecution of faithful Jews by Antiochus Epiphanes, a time when the forces of chaos were again threatening God's people as never before, the visionary sees the chaos monsters arising from the great cosmic ocean (Dan. 7: 2-8). But then he sees an 'enthronement scene' in heaven:

> As I looked, thrones were placed
> and one that was ancient of days took his seat . . .
> his throne was fiery flames,
> its wheels burning fire . . . . (v. 9)

God's kingly rule is asserted as he breaks the power of the beasts representing the pagan, persecuting world empires which are in rebellion against his sovereignty:

> And as I looked the beast was slain, and its body destroyed and given over to be burned with fire. As for the rest of the beasts, their dominion was taken away . . . . (vv. 11b, 12a)

In their place the 'Kingdom of God' comes, pictured, in contrast to the 'beasts' of the evil, this-worldly empires, by a human figure:

> and behold, with the clouds of heaven
> there came one like a son of man,
> and he came to the Ancient of Days
> and was presented before him.
> And to him was given dominion and glory and kingdom,
> that all peoples, nations and languages should serve him;
> his dominion is an everlasting dominion,
> which shall not pass away,
> and his kingdom one
> that shall not be destroyed. (vv. 13f.)

This, it turns out, symbolises the rule of the people of God (v. 27). So God's victory over the forces of chaos and evil results in peace, order, victory and salvation for his people as they enter into the fruits of his victory and 'inherit' God's kingdom.

It was natural that, with all the disappointments of history, and repeated experiences of times of suffering and distress, the idea of God's 'kingdom' should take often the form of a future hope and longing. There were those, however, even in the difficult post-exilic period, who saw God's kingdom not just as a future, Utopian hope. There is a 'here-and-now' quality about it, even if his people's present experience is limited and incomplete. The Chronicler uses the term 'kingdom of God' significantly of the period of the historic monarchy in Israel, and employs a striking phrase to describe those times; the rule of the Davidic king is spoken of as 'the kingdom of the LORD in the hands of the sons of David' (II Chr. 13: 8). Solomon sits on a throne of splendour, but it is a splendour that is 'the throne of the kingdom of the LORD over Israel' (I Chr. 28: 5). David, in his prayer, acknowledges that the kingdom is not really his at all:

> 'Thine, O LORD, is the greatness, and the power, and the glory, and the victory, and the majesty; for all that is in the heavens and in the earth is thine; *thine is the kingdom.*' (I Chr. 29: 11)

The Chronicler wrote in the post-exilic period when the monarchy was no more. Ostensibly he is telling the history of the pre-exilic kingdom of the House of David. Yet he makes clear that the promise to David and the purpose of God with his line of descendants was for the building of the temple and the institution of its worship and priestly orders. So, when David tells the elders and people that God had chosen the tribe of Judah from all Israel, the family of Jesse from all Judah, himself from the family of Jesse and, from all his sons, Solomon, the purpose of this whole divine choice was 'to build my house and my courts' (I Chr. 28: 2-8). In the Chronicler's picture of David, David is no longer primarily soldier and political leader, but a second Moses to whom God gave all the instructions for the building of the temple, its worship and its sacral personnel. In other words, the 'Messianic hope' is not to be seen in political, nationalistic and militaristic terms, but as that which finds fulfilment in the emergence of the temple community of the post-exilic period, the 'theocracy'. So whatever future fulfilment of the old promises to David and the nation might be hoped for, God is *now* reigning as king among his people. They do not have to wait for some future eschatological 'day of the LORD' to know him as king. He rules among them in the present. Here and now they are called to be his loyal sub-jects, obedient to his commands, worshipping him and trusting him for all their needs. Amid all the inconsistencies, compromise and half-truths of present history, God rules as king. It is as important to be obedient to him in the present as to look for his ultimate triumph in a new age 'at the end of time'.

Despite the fact, then, that kingship had dubious and disputed roots in Israel, and despite all the different responses it aroused, the concept of God as king proved a fruitful and inspiring one, which far outlived the end of monarchy itself as an institution. It spoke to his people of God's power over chaos and evil, manifested in creation and again at the crisis points of their history. It assured them of his power and care as 'light' and 'life' of his subjects which was the theme not only of their praise but the ground of confidence of their prayers. It assured them that they had in their midst a power working for righteousness, one who could be swift and sure in his judgement of the oppressor and wrongdoer, and strong in the defence of the exploited and the weak. It was, especially in times of disaster and danger, a source of hope for the future, yet even now a present reality, summoning them to the life of obedience, worship and faith. Those who yielded Yahweh their loyal allegiance as subjects could count on living under the protection of his power and justice and the assurance of present and future salvation. The King of Israel, that often depressed and persecuted minority, is the King of all the earth and lord of all time and destiny.

> The LORD, the Most High is terrible,
> a great king over all the earth. (Ps. 47: 2)

Yet . . .

> He chose our heritage for us,
> the pride of Jacob whom he loves. (v. 4)

No wonder such a psalm opens with the call

> Clap your hands, all peoples!
> Shout to God with loud songs of joy!' (v. 1)

It would be good to think that 'all peoples' really meant what it said. For, while the kingship of God can, and did, seem a haven for nationalism, at its best the thought of God as *universal* king is a reminder that he will claim all peoples as his subjects and offer to all the benefits of his reign:

> And the LORD will become king over all the earth . . . Then every one that survives of all the nations that have come to

Jerusalem shall go up year after year to worship the King, the LORD of hosts . . . .' (Zech. 9: 9,16)

NOTES TO CHAPTER FIVE

1. All quotations from Egyptian, Babylonian and Ugaritic texts in this chapter come from J.B. Pritchard (ed.), *Ancient Near Eastern Texts* (see ch. 3 above, n. 4).

2. See chapter 3 above, n. 5. A recent study of this conflict as it is found in the Ugaritic Texts and its influence on the Old Testament is that of J. Day, *God's Conflict with the Dragon and the Sea*, Cambridge, 1985.

3. For an explanation of the 'Deuteronomists' see ch. 2 above n. 2.

4. Abimelech's question to the men of Shechem (Ju. 9: 2) also implies that, at a later stage, the sons of Jerubba'al (apparently another name for Gideon) *were* acting as a ruling family.

5. The Book of Hosea, in its final form, sees the renewal of the Davidic kingship as part of its future hope (3: 5). That, however, belongs to a later stage of Judean editing when the tradents of the Hosea tradition were relating Hosea's preaching to their own contemporaries and compatriots in the southern kingdom.

6. The historians have presented the story of Solomon in such a way that all the traditions about his wealth, wisdom and power come before their notice in I Ki. 11: 1-8 of his sin in marrying foreign wives. All record of the signs of God's displeasure and judgement come after this.

7. Exod. 15: 18, 19: 6, Nu. 23: 21, Deut. 33: 5.

8. This was strongly urged, among others, by M. Buber, *Kingship of God*, the English translation of the 3rd. edition of the German *Königtum Gottes*, London, 1967, esp. pp. 99-107.

9. K.C. Whitelam in *The Just King*, Sheffield, 1979, p. 88. The book is a study of the judicial role of the king in ancient Israel.

10. The word rendered 'inspired decisions' by RSV actually means 'divination', a practice normally disapproved of in the Old Testament. However, the second part of the verse makes it clear that it is the king's *legal* decisions which are being spoken of here. The verse, taken as a whole, probably means that judgement given by a king is as sound and infallible as an oracle given by a prophet.

11. In the Canaanite religious epics the name of the monster conquered by Ba'al is Lotan. 'Leviathan' (see also Isa. 27: 1) seems to be the Hebrew form of that name. In the Babylonian epic the name of the chaos monster was Tiamat. In Genesis 1: 2 we read, 'Darkness was upon the face of the deep'. The Hebrew word for 'deep', *tehôm*, is believed by many scholars to be related etymologically to the word *Tiamat*. It is clear that the myth was known to the Hebrews in various forms (e.g. Ps. 89: 9f., Isa. 51: 9-11). Some scholars have argued that references such as those cited above and in Ps. 74: 12-17, which celebrate the kingship of Yahweh, accompanied a liturgical re-enactment of a mythical battle such as that enacted in the Babylonian New Year Festival. They believe that the psalms which celebrate the fact that 'Yahweh is king' correspond to the cry of victory in the Babylonian festival which announced that 'Marduk is king'. Some believe that the king in Israel played a central role in this festival in the same way that the king did in the Babylonian festival. The whole matter is discussed in A.R. Johnson, *Sacral Kingship in Ancient Israel*, 2nd. ed. Cardiff, 1967 and John Day, *God's Conflict with the Dragon and the Sea*, Cambridge, 1985.

12. e.g. Pss. 29, 47, 93, 95, 96, 97, 98, 99. These are often referred to as 'Enthronement Psalms' by those who believe that they accompanied a liturgical re-enactment of God's victory over the forces of chaos at creation. See previous note.

VI

GOD AS JUDGE

Most of us would rather steer clear of judges. To appear before a judge is usually to be in danger of punishment or involved in costly litigation. Individual judges may be pleasant enough as people but their office has negative associations for many. To call attention to the Old Testament picture of God as 'judge', therefore, may not seem a very attractive exercise. Lurking near is the spectre of the popular suspicion that the Old Testament presents us with a grim God who dispenses judgement and punishment, while the God of the New Testament is a God of love and grace who delights in forgiveness. Both of these, taken alone, are false cardboard cut-outs rather than 'pictures'. There is plenty about the judgement of God in the New Testament and a great deal about the love and forgiveness of God in the Old. Nevertheless, the picture of God as judge is hardly likely to rank as a favourite.

If that is so, many of the Old Testament references to God as judge will come as a shock. For, as often as not, the Israelites are delighting in the picture when they use it. It occurs over and over again in their praise, and is the basis of many of their prayers. For example,

> The heavens declare his righteousness,
> for God himself is judge! (Ps. 50: 6)
> Rise up, O judge of the earth;
> render to the proud their deserts! (Ps. 94: 2)

To understand this we must ask first, as we have done with other pictures of God, what the term 'judge' meant to the people of the Old Testament. In one of the accounts of the rise of the monarchy in Israel, the people said,

> No, but we will have a king over us, that we also may be like all the nations, and that our king may govern (Heb. *shāphat*, 'to judge') us and go out before us and fight our battles. (I Sam. 8: 19f.)

Tradition tells us that they had 'judges' before that, local figures whose rule and administration of justice probably extended only over the area of a tribe or a coalition of towns. Doubtless, therefore, the administration of justice in their hands could be variable and arbitrary and, anyway, the need would be felt increasingly for some more central administration of justice in larger disputes between tribes or individuals from widely separated localities. Tradition remembered abuse of power by local representatives. It told how Samuel appointed his sons as judges but we read that they 'turned aside after gain; they took bribes and perverted justice' (I Sam. 8: 3. The Hebrew word for 'justice' is *mishpāt*, a noun derived from the verb *shāphat*, 'to judge'). This description of Samuel's sons is in direct contrast to the laws which warned judges against 'perverting justice' (e.g. Deut. 16: 19).

Even after the institution of the monarchy local affairs were in the hands of local administrators, often referred to as the 'elders' of a town. Their role in justice (or their failure to dispense justice) is illustrated in the story of Jezebel's 'framing' of Naboth by the bringing of false witnesses to appear before the 'elders' and 'nobles' of Naboth's town (I Ki. 21: 8-14). Gradually, the administration of justice would have become more centralised, however, and both Jehoshaphat (I Ki. 22f.) and Josiah (II Chr. 19) are credited with reforms to this end. The king, then, was the final court of appeal for the ordinary citizen and it was thus vital that he administered justice fairly, especially in the interests of the poor and weak members of society who could not afford the bribes by which the wealthy managed to secure favourable verdicts in the courts.

We have already seen how Absalom could capitalise on David's apparent failure to hear all who carried appeals to him (II Sam. 15: 3-6)[1]. In retrospect, many saw in Solomon the ideal king who prayed to God, not for wealth, military victory or length of life, but the wisdom to 'judge' God's people and 'to discern between good and evil', for who could cope with the task of 'judging this thy great people' without such super-human wisdom? (I Ki. 3: 7-9). This is likely to have been a piece of royal court propaganda for, in fact, Solomon showed remarkably little 'wisdom' in his reign. By his grandiose building programme and luxurious court life-style he imposed great financial burdens and the hated pressed labour-force on his subjects so that his reign was remembered as an oppressive and burdensome one, a major cause of the division of the kingdom after his death (I Ki. 12: 1-16). Nevertheless, the tradition shows what the ideal of kingship was held to be. This is expressed in the 'royal psalms':

> Give the king thy justice, O God,
> and thy righteousness to the royal son!
> May he judge thy people with righteousness,
> and thy poor with justice! (Ps. 72: 1f.)

In those lines the noun *mishpāt* ('justice') is used,[2] and both times paralleled to 'righteousness'. *Mishpāt* comes from the verb 'to judge' and is sometimes translated as 'judgement' or, as here in the RSV, 'justice'. A very interesting occurrence of it, which throws light on its use, is found in Judges chapter 13 when the angel appears to Manoah to announce the miraculous birth of Samson. Manoah asks the angel, 'What is the boy's *mishpāt* to be and what is he to do?' (v. 12). *Mishpāt* can only be translated here, 'manner of life'. 'How are we to bring him up?' is the question. 'By what rule of life is he to be trained to live?'

The king and the judge are called upon to establish *mishpāt*, that is, the way of life based on God's laws. To do that is to 'judge' rightly. The Servant's calling was to bring forth *mishpāt* for the nations (Isa. 42: 1) and he would succeed in establishing *mishpāt* in the earth (v. 4). David was remembered as establishing *mishpāt* in the realm - he did *mishpāt* and righteousness 'for all his people', according to II Samuel 8: 15.

The law itself was aimed at establishing God's *mishpāt*. With regard to this, a revealing phrase occurs twice in the law. Regarding the law of inheritance it is said that it shall be for the Israelites 'a statute of *mishpāt* as the LORD commanded Moses'

(Nu. 27: 11). And concerning the law of the death penalty for murder the same phrase is used in Numbers 35: 29. It is possible that this phrase means merely 'it is to be a customary statute for Israel'. But, equally, it may have the overtone, 'It is a statute aimed at establishing *mishpāt* in Israel'. All God's law is the basis for establishing the way of life God wants his people to have, whether that be the life of an individual or the life of the nation. Further, it is to establish God's way of life in the nation that the king is responsible. He must therefore rule 'rightly' in accordance with God's laws.

The reality must often have seemed to conflict with the ideal, however. This is shown, not only by the prophetic narratives, like those of Nathan confronting David over the affair with Bathsheba (II Sam. 11f.), or Elijah facing Ahab with his annexing of Naboth's vineyard with Jezebel's connivance (I Ki. c.21), but also by the mounting prophetic attacks against the injustice and corruption which were allowed to continue in the kingdoms. Not all kings were evil, of course. Jeremiah can speak of Jehoiachin favourably. Admonishing his son, Jehoiachim, he says:

> Did not your father eat and drink
> and do justice (*mishpāt*) and righteousness?
> Then it was well with him.
> He judged the cause of the poor and needy . . . (Jer. 22: 15f.)

Nevertheless this is in a context of bitter invective against Jehoiakim himself:

> Woe to him who builds his house by unrighteousness
> [lit. in *not*-righteousness]
> and his upper rooms by injustice
> [lit. by *not-mishpāt*];
> who makes his neighbour serve him for nothing,
> and does not give him his wages. (22: 13)

Elsewhere Jeremiah spells out what he means by *mishpāt*:

> Hear the word of the LORD, O house of David!
> Thus says the LORD:
> 'Execute justice (*mishpāt*) in the morning,

and deliver from the hand of the oppressor
him who has been robbed . . . . ' (21: 12f.)

Such an attack he extends to other powerful and wealthy leaders in the country:

> . . . therefore they have become great and rich,
> they have grown fat and sleek . . .
> they judge not with justice (*mishpāṭ*)
> the cause of the fatherless, to make it prosper,
> and they do not defend the rights of the needy. (5: 28)

Earlier, in the eighth century Micah had also attacked the leaders in similar terms:

> Hear this, you heads of the house of Jacob
> and rulers of the house of Israel;
> who abhor justice (*mishpāṭ*)
> and pervert all equity,
> who build Zion with blood
> and Jerusalem with wrong.
> Its heads give judgement (lit. 'judge') for a bribe,
> its priests teach for hire,
> its prophets divine for money . . . . (3: 9-11a).

Amos's well-known attacks on society in the northern kingdom of Israel in the same century show things were no better there:

> Seek the LORD and live,
> lest he break out like a fire in the house of Joseph,
> and it devour, with none to quench it for Bethel,
> O you who turn justice (*mishpāṭ*) to wormwood,
> and cast down righteousness to the earth! (Am. 5: 6f.)

Or again,

> Seek good, and not evil,
> that you may live . . .
> Hate evil, and love good,
> and establish justice (*mishpāṭ*) in the gate . . . . (5: 14f.)

With all this (and there is much more in the same vein in the words of the prophets) one can begin to understand how the weight of injustice and corruption, extortion and oppression could bear down as a crippling burden on those at the bottom of the pile. It is not hard to see that for the poor, and so defenceless, victims of injustice, the thought of a 'judge' who would secure a way of life based on God's law, a 'righteous' order in which the wicked were punished and the weak gained their rights, would be an extremely welcome one. Indeed, we can understand how the verb 'to judge' could even have the overtones of 'deliverance'. So, after Absalom's rebellion had been quelled, the Cushite could say to David,

> 'Good tidings for my lord the king! For the LORD has delivered you [lit. *judged* you] this day from the power of all who rose up against you.' (II Sam. 18: 31)

In such a context, the rendering 'the LORD has delivered you . . . ' is apt; by defeating David's enemies Yahweh had given divine *judgement* in his favour against those who had wronged him. That is why NEB rightly translates this, 'The LORD has avenged you.'

We can now understand how the longing for such a state of affairs could express itself in various ways. We have seen already that disillusionment with the present order of indifference to the poor and injustice for the weak could lend a romantic halo to the memory of great kings of the past. Solomon, in particular, could gather to himself in the memory of tradition the reputation for a super-human wisdom. David also was remembered as one who 'did *mishpāt*'. A poem attributed to him records his saying,

> When one rules justly over men,
> ruling in the fear of God,
> he dawns on them like the morning light . . . . (II Sam. 23: 3b,4a)

It was not only in nostalgia for the past but in hope for the future that the sense of present injustice could express itself. In this respect, some of the prophetic oracles looked for the coming of 'another' David, a faithful representative of the line who would fulfil its true calling.

> For to us a child is born,[3]
> to us a son is given . . .
> Of the increase of his government and of peace
> there will be no end,
> upon the throne of David, and over his kingdom,
> to establish it, and to uphold it
> with justice (*mishpāt*) and righteousness,
> from this time forth and for evermore. (Isa. 9: 6f.)

The 'rightness' of this future king's judgement is even more explicit in another passage in Isaiah:

> He shall not judge by what his eyes see,
> or decide by what his ears hear:
> [i.e. he will not be deceived by false witnesses or
> blinded by a bribe]
> but with righteousness he shall judge the poor,
> and decide with equity for the meek of the earth;
> and he shall smite the earth with the rod of his mouth,
> and with the breath of his lips he shall slay the wicked. (Isa. 11: 3b, 4).

He will truly fulfil the role Solomon was believed to have played in the kingdom for he will display those very qualities for which Solomon prayed in order that he might 'judge' rightly:

> And the Spirit of the LORD shall rest upon him,
> the spirit of wisdom and understanding,
> the spirit of counsel and might,
> the spirit of knowledge and the fear of the LORD. (v. 2)

Solomon had prayed, 'Give thy servant therefore an understanding mind to govern (Heb. *shāphat*) thy people, that I may discern between good and evil; for who is able to govern this great people?' (I Ki. 3: 9). A judge who sees what is really going on and will make no compromises of expediency in his judgement of wickedness when it is cloaked by power and wealth, is a welcome gift to the poor and oppressed. It is this fact which enables us to see with what joy and hope the downtrodden would reach for the idea that God himself is just such a judge.

....

The belief that God is the ultimate and faithful judge who is determined to establish *mishpāt* in society is a source of constant joy in the Old Testament. No evil-doers are too strong to oppose him. No one can deceive him nor blur his judgement by bribery. He will champion the cause of the poor and needy. His justice is perfect, his judgements all-wise. For the widow, the orphan, the poor and the immigrant, the God who is judge is in a real sense the God who is their deliverer.

Such confidence breathes through the laments of the sufferer:

'O LORD, thou wilt hear the desire of the meek;
thou wilt strengthen their heart,
thou wilt incline thine ear
to do justice to the fatherless and the oppressed,
so that the man who is of the earth
may strike terror no more.' (Ps. 10: 17f.)

And this immediately follows the triumphant assertion, 'The LORD is king for ever and ever' (v. 16). The writer of Lamentations similarly finds in God a last court of appeal when no other redress is available:

Thou hast taken up my cause, O Lord,
thou hast redeemed my life.
Thou hast seen the wrong done to me, O LORD;
judge thou my cause. (Lam. 3: 58).

The chief cause of the confidence behind such prayers is the righteousness of God as judge:

The LORD judges the peoples;
judge me, O LORD, according to my righteousness
and according to the integrity that is in me; (Ps. 7: 8)

for

> God is a righteous judge,
> and a God who has indignation every day. (v. 11)

Similar petitions are heard in many Psalms (e.g. Pss. 26: 1, 35: 24, 43: 1). Indeed, this raises a vital point. Only if God is a God who does punish wickedness, who does 'have indignation every day' can he really be a righteous God, a power making for righteousness and *mishpāt* in the earth. A God who never judged could never be the ground of trust nor the deliverer of the poor and oppressed. For the Old Testament this is an attribute of God which is at the heart of faith, worship and hope. It is only thus that the oppressed will be able to say,

> Surely there is a reward for the righteous;
> surely there is a God who judges on earth. (Ps. 58: 11)

It is, however, not always evident in experience that God does judge, dealing out reward for the righteous, acquitting the innocent and exposing the guilty by awarding punishment for their sin. Often the guilty seem to get off 'scot free' as we say, while the innocent know oppression and suffering. This universal feeling is expressed especially in the Psalms of lament where the worshipper cries out to God to redress the balance. So one Psalmist declares his moral innocence before God:

> O LORD my God, if I have done this,
> if there is wrong in my hands,
> if I have requited my friend with evil
> or plundered my enemy without cause,
> let the enemy pursue me and overtake me . . . . (Ps. 7: 3-5)

This leads to a prayer for God to act:

> Arise, O LORD, in thy anger,
> lift thyself up against the fury of my enemies;
> awake O God; thou hast appointed a judgement. (v. 6)

He seems confident that God will do this since God 'is a righteous judge' (v. 11). But there were clearly times when Israelites were less sure. The prophet of the exile, so-called 'Second Isaiah', obviously addresses the laments with which they were crying out to God when he says:

> Why do you say, O Jacob,
> and speak, O Israel,
> 'My way is hid from the LORD,
> and my *mishpāt* is disregarded by my God?' (Isa. 40: 27)

Jeremiah, in a remarkable series of laments, also questions the delay in God's action as a righteous judge.[4] After complaining of the hostility of his hearers, he goes on to say,

> But, O LORD of hosts, who judgest righteously,
> who triest the heart and the mind,
> let me see thy vengeance upon them,
> for to thee I have committed my cause. (Jer. 12: 20)

The Hebrew word translated by the RSV there as 'cause' (*rîb*) is one to which we shall have to return. It means 'a legal action' and, in this instance, probably refers to the case Jeremiah has against his powerful and hostile opponents. Here, the mood seems to be one of confident faith, but in 12: 1-6 some of that confidence has evaporated:

> Righteous art thou, O LORD,
> when I complain to thee;
> yet I would plead my case before thee.
> Why does the way of the wicked prosper?
> Why do all who are treacherous thrive? (Jer. 12: 1)

The Hebrew of the phrase 'yet I would plead my case before thee' reads, literally, 'Nevertheless, I will address you over matters of *mishpāt*'. God does not appear to be establishing *mishpāt* in a society in which the wicked thrive.

The clearest example of one who questions the righteousness of God as judge in the Old Testament is Job. The book abounds in legal language and metaphor. This classic case of a righteous man who suffers intensely raises acutely the issue of the righteousness of God. After two speeches which give vent to his dismay at the enormity of his suffering, Job begins with a cry which could be rendered:

> How can a man clear his name before God? (Jb. 9: 2)

The Hebrew verb used here means basically 'to be holy' but it has legal overtones of being 'innocent' or 'in the right', as we might say. Job is convinced that he is 'innocent' and that he has not merited his suffering as a just judgement on sin. Yet how can one hope to establish innocence before God? He continues:

> If one entered into a law-suit with him,
> one could not answer him once in a thousand times. (Jb. 9: 3)

The case would be far too one-sided. It would be like conducting one's own defence against the most skilled barrister. Later in the same speech he returns to this:

> For he is not a man, as I am,
> that I might answer him,
> that we should come together into *mishpāt*. (v. 32)

In this instance the word implies coming into legal dispute to establish what is the 'justice' of the case. There then follows a most remarkable statement:

> For there is no assessor between us,
> who might place his hand on the two of us . . . . (v. 33)

or, as the NEB puts the second line, 'to impose his authority on us both'. God is, in fact, both judge and adversary—a concept the prophets take up—and Job complains that this makes the case unequal and unfair.

Yet, in a strange and difficult passage, it may be that Job sees that the only attorney he could have adequately to plead his case would be God himself, while it is also before God that the argument must be made effective:

> O earth, cover not my blood,
> and let my cry find no resting place. (Jb. 16: 18)

This refers to the idea, expressed in the story of Cain and Abel in Genesis chapter 4 that the blood of a murdered man cries out for vengeance. Such vengeance is the task of his next of kin (for a further exploration of the role of the kinsman, see chapter one above). In Abel's case, since he has been murdered by his next of kin, the blood cries out to God for vengeance.[5] The appeal for such a 'kinsman' to plead Job's own case and vindicate him is taken up again later in 19: 25. But already here the confidence is expressed:

> Even now, behold, my witness is in heaven,
> and he that vouches for me is on high.' (16: 19)

There, in heaven, where it counts, is a true witness, as opposed to the 'false' witnesses (his friends) who accuse him (v. 20). In contrast to any appeal to them, he appeals to God:

> ... my eye pours out tears to God,
> that he would maintain the right of a man with God .... (vv. 20-21)

There we must leave Job, with the penetrating insight that God must be judge and yet only God can mediate effectively for human beings. Job is tossed about between confidence that ultimately God will himself be vindicated as a righteous judge, and despair, like a character in a Kafka novel who doubts whether anyone will ever take any notice of his case. To that extent Job speaks to all people. The book is a striking exploration of the issues raised for faith and doubt, of what it means if God as a righteous judge does, or does not, establish *mishpāt* on earth.

Nor must we miss another remarkable exploration of the theme of God's 'righteousness' as a judge. It occurs in the famous question attributed to Abraham in Genesis 18: 25: 'Shall not the Judge of all earth do right [or, do *mishpāt*]?'[6]

The context is provided by God's threat to destroy Sodom and its inhabitants for their sins. Concerned for his nephew, Lot, and

GOD AS JUDGE

his family who live there (Gen. 13: 12, 19: 1), Abraham questions the justice of destroying a whole city, including both the righteous and the wicked, in one sweeping act of judgement. He intercedes for the city. If there were fifty innocent people there, would God spare it for their sakes? The answer is that God would spare it, and the same answer meets each case Abraham puts to God with increasing boldness. God would not destroy the city if forty-five, forty, thirty, twenty or even ten innocent people were found there. While he is not, apparently, bold enough to press his intercession to its logical conclusion—he never asks if God would spare the city for the sake of one innocent person—the story reflects a questioning of the justice of the kind of theology which is expressed in Deuteronomy 5: 9:

> ... I the LORD your God am a jealous God, visiting the iniquity of the fathers upon the children of the third and fourth generation of those who hate me ...

Such a collective view of punishment is assumed also in the story which saw all Achan's family destroyed for the sin of the one head of the household (Joshua 7, especially vv. 24-26). Perhaps the passage in Genesis 18 reflects the kind of religious sensitivity voiced also in Ezekiel 18: 1-4 (cf. Jer. 31: 29f.):

> The word of the LORD came to me again: 'What do you mean by repeating this proverb concerning the land of Israel, "The fathers have eaten sour grapes, and the children's teeth are set on edge"? As I live, says the Lord GOD, this proverb shall no more be used by you in Israel. Behold all souls are mine; the soul of the father as well as the soul of the son is mine: the soul that sins shall die.'

Perhaps this was the kind of question that arose more and more insistently with the Babylonian exile. Were some to be saved from the destruction of Judah and Jerusalem as a kind of 'remnant' to inherit the promises God had originally made to all Israel? (Cf. Jer. 24, where the exiles whom God sent to Babylon are described as the 'good figs' for whom God had plans of redemption). Could the whole principle of 'collective guilt' work the other way round, and the evil people be spared for the sake of the faithful on the principle of a kind of 'collective righteousness'? Abraham's question is a sounding board for what must often have been the questions of those for whom the inequalities and mysteries of experience obscured the 'rightness' and fairness of God's actions as judge.

One way of slackening the screw, and so easing the tension, between the two apparently irreconcilable opposites of the dogma that God was righteous judge on the one hand, and the evident lack of *mishpāt* in society on the other, was the development of a hope for the future. Here and now, for some reason, the forces of injustice and oppression might seem to be prevailing, but in the future God would act decisively in sovereign justice. He would pass sentence both on the powerful and wicked within Israelite society and on the oppressor nations who violated them from without. Malachi heard some of his contemporaries questioning the justice of God:

> 'Everyone who does evil is good in the sight of the LORD, and he delights in them . . . Where is the God of justice (*mishpāt*)?'
> (Mal. 2: 17)

At least part of the prophet's answer is to assert that God will act in the near future:

> 'Then I will draw near to you for judgement (*mishpāt*); I will be a swift witness [the same word as that used by Job in his longing for a 'witness' in heaven, 16: 19] against the sorcerers, against the adulterers, against those who swear falsely, against those who oppress the hireling in his wages, the widow and orphan, against those who thrust aside the sojourner . . . . '
> (Mal. 3: 5).

This hope in a future 'Assize' when the forces of evil will be judged and the innocent acquitted receives a powerful reinforcement from the liturgy of the Jerusalem temple reflected in many Psalms. In the so-called 'Enthronement Psalms' (discussed more fully in the chapter on 'God as King' above) the theme of God as king subduing the forces of evil and chaos is often heard. Whatever the actual liturgical setting of such Psalms the theme is unambiguous enough.

> Say among the nations, 'The LORD reigns!
> Yea, the world is established,
> it shall never be moved;
> he will *judge* the peoples with equity.' (Ps. 96: 10)

The results of this will be the restoration of the realm of nature to its full vigour and fertility, the subduing of the 'peoples' and the establishment of a moral order of righteousness and truth:

> Then shall all the trees of the wood sing for joy
> before the LORD, for he comes,
> for he comes to judge the earth.
> He will judge the world with righteousness,
> and the peoples with his truth.' (vv. 12b,13)

Such a hope inspires the prayer of the people in times of despair:

> Arise, O God, judge the earth;
> for to thee belong all the nations!' (Ps. 82: 8)

So this becomes the hope for the future in some of the exilic and post-exilic prophets who offer assurance to the Israel of the exile, or to those who have returned only to become the subject peoples of the world empire of a greater power. This universal judgement will take place. In answer to the laments of the exiles Second Isaiah assures them:

> Listen to me, my people,
> and give ear to me, my nation;
> for a law will go forth from me,
> and my justice (*mishpāt*) for a light to the peoples.
> My deliverance draws near speedily,
> my salvation has gone forth,
> and my arms [symbol of power and authority] will rule [lit. 'judge'] the peoples. (Isa. 51: 4f.)

In some later post-exilic prophetic literature there is an increasing tendency to equate Israel's national enemies with God's enemies. Often, therefore, pictures of future judgement take on a growing severity in attitude to the 'nations'. So Joel pictures God gathering all the 'nations', symbols of Israel's oppressors, to judge them in the valley of 'Jehoshaphat'—the name means 'God has judged'. The battle becomes symbolic of God's final overthrow of the forces of evil:

> For behold, in those days and at that time, when I restore the fortunes of Judah and Jerusalem, I will gather all the nations and bring them down to the valley of Jehoshaphat, and I will enter into judgement with them there, on account of my people and my heritage Israel, because they have scattered them among the nations, and have divided up my land . . . . (Joel 3: 1f.)

We hear that note again in later chapters of Isaiah:

> For behold, the LORD will come in fire,
> and his chariots like the stormwind,
> to render his anger in fury,
> and his rebuke with flames of fire.
> For by fire will the LORD execute judgement,
> and by his sword, upon all flesh;
> and those slain by the LORD shall be many. (Isa. 66: 15f.)

The 'Zion tradition' of the pre-exilic Jerusalem temple especially could give rise to the smug assurance that God would destroy all their national foes while defending and vindicating them, whatever happened and however they acted. Such hopes did not need to be nationalistic to be exclusive. Those who saw themselves as an oppressed minority within the community could translate their longing for justice all too easily into the belief that it was always *others* who would be the object of God's judgement.

It is against the background of such a danger that we have to see the remarkable use of the picture of God as judge in the main prophetic tradition of the Old Testament. For these prophets God is indeed the righteous judge whose aim is to establish *mishpāt*. To this end he will pass sentence on evil-doers, whoever they prove to be. His own people will know no immunity if, by their conduct, they obstruct his purpose for *mishpāt*. In an ominous play on words Isaiah could express God's attitude to the community of his own people in Judah and Jerusalem in this way:

> ... and he looked for justice [*mishpāt*],
> but behold, bloodshed [*mishpāh*];
> for righteousness [*tsᵉdāqah*],
> but behold, a cry [*tsᵉ'āqah*]! (Isa. 5: 7b)

So he calls on the inhabitants of Judah and Jerusalem to act as witnesses in the case of 'God v. his vineyard (= Israel)':

> And now, O inhabitants of Jerusalem
> and men of Judah,
> judge, I pray you, between me
> and my vineyard. (Isa. 5: 3)

In other words, they are invited to accuse themselves in the name of 'justice'.

The attacks of the pre-exilic prophets on the social corruption of Israelite society are too well-known to need rehearsing here. Yet we should notice that they use courtroom imagery to picture God's action as judge. They use especially the *rîb* (legal dispute) form of invective. God is pictured as litigant, taking his people to court to bring his case against them, the very court in which, as righteous judge, he pronounces sentence against their evil.

> Hear the word of the LORD,
> O people of Israel;
> for the LORD has a controversy (*rîb*)
> with the inhabitants of the land. (Hos. 4: 1)

Having summoned his opponents to the court hearing, the indictment is read out:

> There is no faithfulness or kindness,
> and no knowledge of God in the land;
> there is swearing, lying, killing, stealing and committing adultery;
> they break all bounds and murder follows murder. (vv. 1b-3)

Where, however, we should expect the plea for the defence, it is categorically stated that none is possible:

> Yet let no one contend, and let none accuse . . .' [i.e. accuse the judge of unfairness]. (v. 4)

With the clear evidence that no defence can be offered, sentence is passed:

> You [the priest] shall stumble by day,
> the prophet also shall stumble with you by night;
> and I will destroy your mother . . . . (v. 5)[7]

To us it seems unfair that God should be both prosecutor and judge, and that defence pleas are stifled. One recent writer on the form has argued that this is to show that, in the view of the prophet, there can be and is no defence for a nation which has bred and tolerated such evils.[8] There is no escape from God's judgement against the nation as a whole and, in particular, those who fail by their corrupt and self-seeking misuse of positions of authority and leadership. As judge, God is the 'enduring power, not ourselves, which makes for righteousness'.[9] All which opposes that purpose for righteousness will be judged.

For a final illustration of the picture of God as judge in the Old Testament we can do no better than turn to Psalm 51.

> For I know my transgressions,
> and my sin is ever before me.
> Against thee, thee only have I sinned,
> and done that which is evil in thy sight,
> so that thou art justified in thy sentence
> and blameless in thy judgement.' (Ps. 51: 3-4)

Here, all claims to 'innocence' and 'righteousness' are set aside. The author[10] throws himself upon the righteous judge, who can discern not only the outward act but also the inward disposition of the heart. There is no dissent from the divine verdict, no plea for the defence, no appeal to a higher court, no attempt to appease God with sacrifices (v. 16). Yet, assured of the penetrating insight of God as judge, he knows that part of the 'righteousness' of God is to show mercy. God establishes *mishpāt* in the individual life as in the community, not just by the searing sentence of vengeance, but by the grace which forgives the penitent.

> The sacrifice acceptable to God is a broken spirit; a broken and contrite heart, O God, thou wilt not despise. (v. 17)

To that judge the psalmist confides—not his case, he has none—but himself. God as judge establishes righteousness both by passing sentence on evil but also by showing mercy to the penitent. This is a high note in the picture of God as judge in the Old Testament and a fitting climax with which to conclude our study of it. Here, Abraham's question is answered in the affirmative in the faith of a worshipper. For him, assuredly this judge of all the earth does do right.

NOTES TO CHAPTER SIX

1. See p. 122 above (ch. 5).

2. The first occurrence of the word in the Hebrew text is in the plural and would need to be rendered by 'thy judgements'. However, the singular occurs both in the Septuagint (the Greek Version of the Old Testament) and the Syriac and is to be preferred.

3. Perhaps this oracle related to the birth of a particular son of the Davidic line in Isaiah's lifetime, perhaps Hezekiah. However, the Hebrew prophets could speak of a future action of God as already having happened, so confident were they of its fulfilment. In that case this could be a prediction of something which would happen in an indefinite future, in spite of the tense of the verb.

4. The relevant passages are, Jer. 11: 18-20, 12: 1-6, 15: 10-12, 15-21, 17: 14-18, 20: 7-12, 14-18. There has been considerable discussion on how these 'laments' are to be interpreted. Their very close parallels in vocabulary and structure to the Psalms of Individual Lament have led some to argue that the prophet is here following a set liturgical pattern. He would then in fact be acting as a sanctuary prophet and voicing in the first person the laments of the whole community. Most, however, feel that, while the prophet obviously does speak and pray as represen-

tative of his people and on their behalf, the passages contain elements which are so intensely personal to Jeremiah that we hear in them his own doubts and longings.

5. For further detail, see p. 28 above (ch. 1).

6. This passage, and others which question the integrity of God as a righteous judge, are dealt with more fully by R. Davidson, *The Courage to Doubt*, London, 1983.

7. Other similar passages making use of the *rîb* form of accusation are to be found in Isa. 1: 2f., 3: 13-15, Hos. 2: 4-17 and Ps. 50. In addition, Second Isaiah uses the term to show how God, in his purpose of salvation for his people, brings a legal action against the (false) gods (41: 21-29) and the nations (43: 8-13).

8. K. Nielsen, *Yahweh as Prosecutor and Judge*, JSOT Supp. 9, Sheffield, 1978.

9. Matthew Arnold, *Literature and Dogma: An Essay towards a better Apprehension of the Bible*, 1873. This is cited by A.R. Johnson, *Sacral Kingship in Ancient Israel*, 2nd. ed., Cardiff, 1967, p.13. Johnson's caution about Arnold's general understanding of the nature of God is endorsed by the present writer.

10. Tradition has assigned the psalm to David. Whoever the writer was, he speaks in fact for 'Everyman'.

VII

GOD AS SHEPHERD

The Old Testament picture of God as 'Shepherd' is perhaps the most familiar and honoured of all. Almost everyone knows the 23rd. Psalm with its opening, 'The Lord is my shepherd'. While it would come naturally to a people with a pastoral background it requires little imagination to see its force even by those whose lives are far removed from fields and hills and other places where sheep may safely graze. Yet in the ancient world it was not wholly a pastoral image even if its roots obviously lay there. The word 'shepherd' had political connotations. In particular, it was a well-known designation of the king.

So Hammurabi, the Babylonian king, in his law-code describes himself as 'Hammurabi, the shepherd called by Enlil am I.'[1] In this he was following precedent since a forerunner of his, Lipit-Ishtar, in his law-code which pre-dated that of Hammurabi by more than a century and a half, designates himself, 'I, Lipit-Ishtar, the humble shepherd of Nippur.'[2] Sometimes in the Old Testament 'shepherd' clearly has this political sense. An oracle of Jeremiah's threatening judgement by God against the people of Benjamin, Judah and Jerusalem runs:

> The comely and delicately bred I will destroy,
> the daughter of Zion.
> Shepherds with their flocks shall come against her,
> they shall pasture, each in his place. (Jer. 6: 2f.)

A literal encampment of shepherds would hardly be likely to strike terror into the people's hearts. Jeremiah is clearly predicting an invasion by foreign powers under their kings who will come and drive out the Israelites, taking over their homeland for their own use. This is made explicit in what immediately follows:

> Prepare war against her,
> up, and let us attack at noon! (v. 4)

These words are placed dramatically by the prophet on the lips of those he envisages as coming to attack the city.

Another explicitly political use of the term 'shepherd' is found in Second Isaiah. Just as Isaiah of Jerusalem had seen God to be using a foreign power, Assyria, for his purpose in judging the people (Isa. 10: 5f.) so Second Isaiah sees him to be using another power, the Persians under their leader Cyrus, to secure their release. Speaking of God and his power seen both in creation and over other gods and their spokesmen, as well as in the prophetic word and its fulfilment, he goes on:

> Who says of Cyrus, He is my Shepherd,
> and he shall fulfil all my purpose. (Isa. 44: 28)

That purpose will include the rebuilding of Jerusalem and the temple. Cyrus' kingship is seen to be of Yahweh's appointment, a fact made even more explicit by the extraordinary description of the foreign Cyrus as 'my anointed' (Heb. 'my Messiah'), 'whose right hand I have grasped', i.e. whose power and authority have been directly bestowed by Yahweh (Isa. 45: 1).

This description of the king as a 'shepherd' may help us to understand how it is that the calling of David from his role of 'shepherd' in a literal sense, to be king (i.e. 'shepherd' in a more metaphorical sense) is seen in the Old Testament to be particularly apt. Tradition relates how, when Samuel comes to Bethlehem to meet Jesse and his family to anoint a king, he sees seven of Jesse's sons, none of whom, for all their striking physical appearance, he believes to be the one chosen of God (I Sam. 16: 1-10). 'Are all your sons here?' he asks, to which Jesse replies, 'There remains the youngest, but behold, *he is keeping the sheep*' (v. 11). David was sent for and anointed as the one chosen to be king, that is, 'shepherd' of God s people. Told in this way, this is probably a later form of the story, romanticising David's prior divine election. It certainly serves very conveniently as pro-David propaganda! One must not forget that he had a contender to the throne after Saul's death, namely Ishba'al, who ruled in the north before being be-trayed to David by Abner. David no doubt had to justify his replacement of the house of Saul (II Sam. 2: 8-10, cf. ch. 3). But it may well represent a tradition which saw significance and appropriateness in the two roles. (Indeed, one wonders whether this was a more widespread element of tradition. It is interesting that several other prominent leaders in Israel's history are depicted as having been shepherds, e.g. Joseph in Gen. 37: 2, and Moses in Exod. 3: 1).

The relationship between the two roles of shepherd and king is brought out in the words of God through Nathan, the prophet, when he established the covenant with David and his successors.

> 'In all places where I have moved with all the people of Israel, did I speak a word with any of the judges of Israel, whom I commanded to shepherd my people Israel, saying, "Why have you not built me a house of cedar?" Now therefore thus you shall say to my servant David, "Thus says the LORD of hosts, I took you from the pasture, from following the sheep, that you should be prince over my people Israel . . . ."' (II Sam. 7: 7f.)

Now, David as 'shepherd' of Yahweh's people will fulfil, under God, one of the important functions of a shepherd; he will lead them to a place of peace and security from the enemies who otherwise would ravage the flock. Indeed, how fitting that one who, as shepherd, had fought off the attacks of lions and bears (I Sam. 17: 34ff.) and could therefore dispose of a mere Philistine, however tall and fearful tradition painted Goliath to be, should now be the one who was responsible for fighting off the enemies of God's people. A shepherd had to be tough as well as gentle. That is why the prophet Micah sees the future shepherd/king acting in the *strength* of the LORD.

> And he shall stand and feed his flock in the strength of the LORD,
> in the majesty of the name of the LORD his God.
> And they shall dwell secure,

for now he shall be great
to the ends of the earth. (Mic. 5: 4)

This protective element in a shepherd's role was not lost on the tribes of Israel when they came to Hebron to acknowledge David as their king. They said to him:

> 'In times past, when Saul was king over us, it was you that *led out and brought in* Israel; and the LORD said to you, "You shall be shepherd of my people Israel, and you shall be prince over Israel"'. (II Sam. 5: 2)

'Leading in' and 'leading out' are pastoral images of the shepherd, leading his flock out to nourishing grazing by day and leading them back to the security of the fold at night.

This tradition of the 'shepherd' who became a 'shepherd' was passed on in Israel's worship. In a context of praise and thanksgiving Psalm 78 surveys God's dealings with the nation throughout their history. The climax of it all is found in the choice of David from the tribe of Judah and it brings out the parallel between the two roles of the one who was the divine choice:

> He chose David his servant,
> and took him from the sheepfolds;
> from tending the ewes that had young he brought him
> to be the shepherd of Jacob his people,
> of Israel his inheritance. (Ps. 78: 70f.)

And David showed skill in his monarchic role equal to that which he had shown as shepherd of the flock. RSV misses the force of the verb in what follows and we must render:

> With upright heart he shepherded them,
> and he led them with skilful hand. (v. 72)

So the king, as shepherd, was called to care for God s flock. He was responsible for their material prosperity, which can be described as 'pasturing' them. So, according to Ezekiel, the ideal David of the future will 'feed them':

> and he shall feed them:
> he shall feed them and be their shepherd. (Ezek. 34: 23)

The verb here translated 'feed' is the verb related to the noun 'shepherd' and means 'to shepherd' or 'to pasture'. As we have already noted, Micah sees the role of the future king similarly:

> And he shall stand and feed his flock in the strength of the LORD. (Mic. 5: 4)

Further, the king was to give his people more than mere material prosperity. He was also to instruct the people with wise teaching.

> And I will give you shepherds after my own heart,
> who will feed you with knowledge and understanding. (Jer. 3: 15).

We have already seen that these were the very qualities tradition related Solomon as seeking in his role as king over Israel (I Ki. 3: 9).[3] Again, we have seen how the king was responsible for warding off the attacks of those who aimed to despoil the flock and for guiding them into places of security. The alternative is the 'scattering' of the sheep into places where they will starve for lack of pasture and be vulnerable to attacks by wild beasts. Probably Numbers 27: 16f. has monarchy in mind when it describes the role of Joshua as leader:

> Let the LORD, the God of the spirits of all flesh, appoint a man over the congregation, who shall go out before them and come in before them, who shall lead them out and bring them in; that the congregation of the LORD may not be as sheep which have no shepherd.

It is very possible that this passage has influenced the New Testament picture of Jesus as 'the Good Shepherd', especially in John 10: 3f., 9. More immediately, one recalls the dire prediction of Micaiah that if Ahab and Jehoshaphat, the kings of Israel and Judah, persist in their design to attack the Syrians against the word of God revealed to him as a true prophet, they and their people face death and defeat:

I saw all Israel scattered upon the mountains, as sheep that have no shepherd. (I Ki. 22: 17)

Indeed, it is ironic that we can see what was expected of the king as 'shepherd' by the fierce *attacks* of the seventh century and exilic prophets against those whom they described as 'false shepherds'. They were the ones who had led Israel astray and so brought about the destruction of their safe dwelling place in the land and their spoliation by foreign powers. Such attacks figure most prominently, although not exclusively, in the books of Jeremiah and Ezekiel. It is very likely that, in some of these passages, the term 'shepherd' has acquired a wider connotation than that specifically of kingship. Often, prophets, priests and other leaders are included in the denunciations. These passages may represent some move in the period of the exile to blame the former leaders rather than the whole nation for the disaster that had happened. Perhaps this was an attempt to redress the balance from the earlier prophets who appear often to have predicted judgement on all the community generally, rather than singling out the wicked among them alone. However, there is no doubt that all have been involved in the consequences of such betrayal of trust by those whom God had appointed as 'shepherd' over his people.

This becomes clear in several passages. One of these, attacking the 'false shepherds' is found in Ezekiel 34: 1-10. The shepherds are accused of having fed themselves rather than the sheep (vv. 2, 3, 8b). They have used their position to serve self-advancement and private gain without care for the well-being of those committed to their charge. Indeed, they have exploited them, gaining their wealth by taxation and private use of public funds in the way shepherds might seek to gain profit from a flock of sheep by sale of the fleeces and their flesh for meat while neglecting the welfare of the sheep themselves. They have not 'strengthened the weak', 'healed the sick', or 'bound up the crippled'. These charges remind us that the king's first responsibility was to secure justice for the weak and oppressed members of society. In the pastoral imagery of this passage they are charged with neglecting this first charge on their efforts. They have not brought back those who have strayed or sought the lost.

GOD AS SHEPHERD

Perhaps, in the continuation of the imagery, this is a reference to their failure to uphold the cause of true Yahwistic faith against the inroads of foreign religious influence which proved so seductive to many in Israel. This is the more likely since religious apostasy is Ezekiel's first accusation against the nation.

All this parallels the repeated attacks against 'false shepherds' found in the Book of Jeremiah:

> 'Woe to the shepherds who destroy and scatter the sheep of my pasture!' says the LORD, the God of Israel, concerning the shepherds who care for my people: 'You have scattered my flock and driven them away, and you have not attended to them. Behold, I will attend to you for your evil doings,' says the LORD. 'Then I will gather the remnant of my flock out of all the countries where I have driven them, and I will bring them to their fold, and they shall be fruitful and multiply. I will set shepherds over them who will care for them, and they shall fear no more, nor be dismayed, neither shall any be missing,' says the LORD. (Jer. 23: 1-4)

The play on words which RSV renders as 'to attend' could equally well be translated, 'they have not *visited* the flock (in care) . . . therefore I (God) will *visit* them (the shepherds) in punishment.'

Another passage records an attack on all sections of the leaders of the people:

> The priests did not say, 'Where is the LORD?'
> Those who handle the law did not know me;
> the 'shepherds' [RSV rulers] transgressed against me;
> the prophets prophesied by Ba'al,
> and went after things that do not profit. (Jer. 2: 8)

All these went their own way without 'seeking' God's direction or help:

> For the shepherds are stupid,
> and do not inquire of [seek] the LORD;
> therefore they have not prospered,
> and all their flock is scattered. (Jer. 10: 21)

It is ironic that those who did not seek Yahweh also failed to 'seek' the sheep. Indeed, because of the judgement which has come upon the city and its people, its captors said, with a fine irony,

> 'It is Zion, for whom no one seeks.' (Jer. 30: 17)

. . . .

In the face of this failure of the historic line of 'shepherd' leading to the disaster of the exile, God's response is two-fold. He himself is going to act as the 'Shepherd' of Israel and, according to some traditions at least, will again raise up shepherds who will be faithful in the discharge of their office.

So, following the passage in which Jeremiah had announced that God would 'visit' the shepherds who had not visited the flock, God continues:

> Then I will gather the remnant of my flock out of all countries where I have driven them, and will bring them back . . . I will set shepherds over them who will care for them . . . neither shall any of them be missing. (Jer. 23: 3f.)

The last verb rendered as 'be missing' represents a word-play on the verb to 'visit' which had already been used in two senses in the first two verses. None of the restored flock would, literally, 'be visited', i.e. in judgement. It may be, as some have argued, that the passive mood of this verb has the overtone of 'going missing', but it could quite appropriately mean that the restored flock would not be 'visited' any more in judgement because faithful shepherds will now be over them who will care for them properly, keeping them in right paths.

Another, obviously exilic pasage in the Book of Jeremiah continues the imagery of the flock and of Yahweh bringing that flock back to safe pastures.

> Israel is a hunted sheep, driven away by lions. First the king of Assyria devoured him, and now at last Nebuchadrezzar king of Babylon has gnawed his bones . . . I will restore Israel to his

GOD AS SHEPHERD

pasture, and he shall feed on Carmel and in Bashan, and his desire shall be satisfied . . . . (Jer. 50: 17, 19)

Or, as it is expressed elsewhere in the book:

> He who scattered Israel will gather him,
> and will keep him as a shepherd keeps his flock. (Jer. 31: 10)

Perhaps one of the most charming and idyllic pictures of God bringing his people back from exile like a shepherd leading his flock is provided by Second Isaiah:

> He will feed his flock like a shepherd,
> he will gather the lambs in his arms,
> he will carry them in his bosom,
> and gently lead those that are with young. (Isa. 41: 11)

Gentle as the picture is, however, it does not ignore a necessary factor for any successful shepherd which we have noted earlier. The shepherd must have strength. These words immediately precede those just quoted:

> Behold, the Lord GOD comes with might,
> and his arm rules for him. (Isa. 41: 10a)

It is Ezekiel again who gives us the most detailed contrast to the false shepherds with his picture of the saving acts of God as 'Shepherd'. As shepherd he is all that those false shepherds failed to be:

> For thus says the Lord GOD: 'Behold, I, I myself will search for my sheep, and will seek them out. As a shepherd seeks out his flock when some of his sheep have been scattered abroad, so I will seek out my sheep; and I will rescue them from all places where they have been scattered on a day of clouds and thick darkness . . . and I will feed them on the mountains of Israel, by the fountains, and in all the inhabited places of the country . . . I myself will be shepherd of my sheep, and I will make them lie down,' says the Lord GOD. 'I will seek the lost, and I will bring back the strayed, and I will bind up the crippled, and

I will strengthen the weak, and the fat and the strong I will watch over;[4] I will feed them in justice.' (Ezek. 34: 11-16)

This last concept of 'justice' (*mishpāt*) makes the link again between 'shepherd' and 'king'. The Divine King will rule as the ideal shepherd and by his reign will achieve *mishpāt*. Indeed, in an expansion of the material in chapter 34, an interesting new note is introduced. God himself will judge fairly between the oppressors in the community and the weak and defenceless victims.

> Behold, I, I myself, will judge between the fat sheep and the lean sheep. Because you push with side and shoulder, and thrust at all the weak with your horns, till you have scattered them abroad, I will save my flock, they shall no longer be a prey; and I will judge between sheep and sheep. (vv. 20-22)

It may seem strange that a passage which thus announces so emphatically that God himself will act as shepherd to his sheep in contrast to the false shepherds, nevertheless carries a postscript saying that he will set 'my servant David' over them as shepherd (vv. 23-24). It can be debated whether this, and its related passage in 37: 24-28 are original to Ezekiel or not. Yet we have seen in the Book of Jeremiah that the two ideas can be brought together. God will act as shepherd himself and *also* raise up faithful shepherds. This appeared to arouse no sense of ambiguity or inconsistency. It is noteworthy that, here in Ezekiel, David is not called 'king' but rather 'prince', both here and in 37: 24-28. Further, in chapters 40-48 the leader is also called 'prince' rather than 'king' (e.g. 45: 7-9). In this last passage there is a strong warning against repeating the oppression and injustice that so often characterised the rule of their forerunners in the pre-exilic days. All we can say here about the place of the king in the post-exilic community 'shepherded' by God himself, is that there appear to have been differences of opinion about the organization of the life of the community after the exile. Some believed that the Davidic dynasty would be renewed. Others, cautiously, saw that its role would have to be modified. Others, like Second Isaiah, maintain a deafening silence on the subject.

The theme of God the Shepherd provided not only ground for hope for the future, but material for praise. Psalm 95 opens with a call to worship, proclaiming God's universal kingship, he who is the creator of all:

> O come, let us sing to the LORD;
> let us make a joyful noise to the rock of our
> salvation! . . .
> For the LORD is a great God,
> and a great King above all gods.
> In his hands are the depths of the earth;
> the heights of the mountains are his also.
> The sea is his, for he made it;
> for his hands formed the dry land.' (vv. 1, 3-5)

But again, the concept of kingship is linked with that of shepherd. So the Psalm moves into a second call to worship expressing this:

> O come, let us worship and bow down,
> let us kneel before the LORD, our Maker!
> For he is our God,
> and we are the people of his pasture,
> and the sheep of his hand.' (vv. 6f.)

In this case the idea forms the basis of a call to obedience. The sheep must follow the shepherd if he is to fulfil his function of leading them in to the place of shelter and pasturage. Their forefathers forgot this after the Exodus and, as a result, wandered for forty years in the wilderness without finding a fold.

> O that today you would hearken to his voice!
> Harden not your hearts, as at Meribah,
> as on the day at Massah in the wilderness,
> when your fathers tested me . . .
> For forty years I loathed that generation,
> and said, 'They are a people who err in heart,
> and they do not regard my ways.'
> Therefore I swore in my anger
> that they should not enter my rest. (vv. 7b-11)

Similarly, Psalm 100 is a joyous celebration of God as Shepherd:

> Make a joyful noise to the LORD, all the lands!
> Serve the LORD with gladness!
> Come into his presence with singing!
> Know that the LORD is God!
> It is he that made us, and we are his,
> we are his people, and the sheep of his pasture.
> For the LORD is good;
> his steadfast love endures for ever,
> and his faithfulness to all generations.

Not only does the concept furnish material for praise but is the basis for prayer in time of distress. The worshippers throw themselves on the gentle mercy and protection of the shepherd.

> Give ear, O Shepherd of Israel,
> thou who leadest Joseph like a flock! (Ps. 80: 1a)

This 'Shepherd' is, of course, the divine King, and therefore has the strength to be an effective shepherd:

> Thou who art enthroned upon the cherubim,
> shine forth . . .
> Stir up thy might,
> come and save us! (vv. 1bf.)

Again, Psalm 28 is a lament, perhaps uttered by the human king as representative of his people in a time of distress. It concludes with an affirmation and a petition:

> The LORD is the strength of his people,
> he is the saving refuge of his anointed.
> O save thy people, and bless thy heritage;
> be thou their *shepherd*, and carry them for ever. (vv. 8-9)

We have left to the last the most celebrated affirmation of God as Shepherd, Psalm 23, where an individual has appropriated as his own the national faith that God is shepherd of his people, Israel. It is noteworthy how this echoes so many of the themes

GOD AS SHEPHERD

of the passage in Ezekiel 34 in which God describes himself as the good shepherd. He rescues the sheep from all places where they have been scattered on a day of cloud and thick darkness. So, in Psalm 23, in different words the same idea is echoed. He accompanies his flock through the valley of 'deep darkness'. He leads the flock to where there is pasture, concerned to feed *them*, not himself. He leads and guides his flock on those right paths that lead to shelter and security. In the place of danger he is present to defend the weak and helpless. He searches for them to bring them home to his own household. The Psalm forms a fitting climax to our study of what it meant for the people of Israel to be championed by a God who could fittingly be described as 'Shepherd'. For the sake of freshness we cite the translation of it by A.R. Johnson.[5]

> With Yahweh as my Shepherd there is nothing that I lack;
> he seeth that I lie down where there is grass for pasture.
> He leadeth me where restful water may be found,
> satisfying my need to the full.
> He guideth me along the right tracks,
> thus answering to his name.
> Even if my way lieth through a valley deep in shadow,
> I dread no evil;
> for thou art with me,
> my fears allayed by thy club and thy staff.
> Thou dost show mine enemies
> that I am welcome at thy table,
> pouring oil on my head,
> my cup filled to overflowing.
> Yea, I shall be pursued by unfailing kindness
> every day of my life,
> finding a home in the Household of Yahweh
> for many a long year.

As a postscript it is tempting to ponder whether the writer of Mark's Gospel in his account of the feeding of the five thousand had Psalm 23 in mind. He alone records the apparently trifling detail that Jesus commanded them to sit down on *the green grass* (Mk. 6: 39). Presumably, this must have been near a stream to be so fresh. Thus the Psalmist's confidence that God would enable him to lie down in green pastures and lead him beside still waters is fulfilled. With its evocation of the Last Supper when Jesus, as here, 'blessed' the loaves, 'broke' them and 'gave' them to the disciples (Mk. 6: 41, cf. 14: 22) it also fulfilled the hope that God would prepare a table for his people in the very sight of their enemies. Perhaps Mark, as well as the writer of the Fourth Gospel, saw Jesus as the 'Good Shepherd'.

Of course, here something is added. The bread broken at the Eucharist was a reminder that Jesus, the Good Shepherd, gave his own life for the sheep. Yet even this, while it transcends much of the Old Testament picture of the 'Good Shepherd' was not wholly without earlier hints. Moses 'the shepherd' who was called to lead the 'flock of God' was remembered as having to die outside the land of promise for the sins of the people so that they could enter it (Deut. 4: 22). It was a fitting tradition to be linked with one who is recorded as praying that his name might be 'blotted out' of God's book so that the people might be forgiven (Exod. 32: 32). Further, the four pictures describing the Servant of the LORD in Second Isaiah (Isa. 42: 1-4, 49: 1-6, 50: 4-9, 52: 13 –53: 12), certainly contain 'royal' elements among other aspects. Yet this 'royal' servant is also a 'suffering servant' who suffers for the sins of others, and his suffering is a means by which the apostate, wandering 'many' become 'accounted righteous' (53: 11). In this, as in so much else, the New Testament pictures of Jesus show him to be a fulfilment of images and concepts already present in the Old Testament.

NOTES TO CHAPTER SEVEN

1. Hammurabi was king of Babylon in the 18th. century BCE. Enlil was the name of a storm god, worshipped at Nippur as the god who created the earth out of the waters of chaos. As we have seen his role and title were later transferred to Marduk, the god of Babylon, when this became the chief city of the kingdom. The translation of this and the following text are to be found in J.B. Pritchard (ed.), *Ancient Near Eastern Texts* (see ch. 3, n. 4), pp. 164, 159.

2. Lipit-Ishtar reigned during the first half of the 19th. century BCE. At that time Nippur was the chief city of the kingdom.

3. See above, p. 145 (ch. 6).

4. The Masoretic Text reads 'I will destroy', but a very small emendation involving only the interchange of two letters, which are easily and often confused, would give the sense 'watch over'.

5. See A.R. Johnson, 'Psalm 23 and the Household of Faith', in *Proclamation and Presence: Old Testament Essays in Honour of Gwynne Henton Davies*, ed. J.I Durham & J.R. Porter, London, 1970, p. 271.

VIII

GOD AS WARRIOR

'The LORD is a man of war' (Exod. 15: 3).

So runs a line in one of the songs of the Old Testament, the so-called 'Song of the Sea' which celebrates Yahweh's victory over the Egyptians, when he delivered his people Israel at the Reed Sea. We may, or may not, welcome such a note in the Old Testament, but it is there and represents a very strong line of tradition which sees Yahweh as a 'Warrior-God'. To ignore this picture of God would be to impose our own principles of selection, or our own 'Canon' on the Old Testament, and to miss something of the rounded wholeness of its witness to God. Only by examining this idea of God as 'warrior' shall we be able to appreciate the radical treatment it receives at the hands of the prophets, and the insight of some, at least, that ultimately God's purpose is to establish peace on the earth, a peace which renders warfare obsolete.

The 'Song of the Sea' in Exodus chapter 15 associates Yahweh as warrior with the deliverance of the Israelites from their slavery in Egypt:

> Pharaoh's chariots and his host he cast into the sea;
> and his picked officers are sunk in the Red Sea.[1]
> Thy right hand, O LORD, glorious in power,
> thy right hand, O LORD, shattered the enemy. (vv. 4, 6)

To that poetic celebration of the victory, though of disputed date, we shall return. In the prose account of the Exodus in chapter 14 the motif is also heard. Moses assures the disheartened Israelites who feel themselves trapped between the sea and the pursuing Egyptian army,

> 'Fear not, stand firm, and see the salvation of the LORD which he will work for you today . . . the LORD will fight for you, and you have only to be still.' (Exod. 14: 13f.)

This introduces a theme we shall hear again in this tradition. It is the theme of human trust, almost of passivity in battle. God, as warrior, fights on his people's behalf. This is re-inforced by the words attributed to the Egyptians themselves. Their chariot wheels trapped and clogged in the returning waters, they say:

> 'Let us flee before Israel; for the LORD fights for them against the Egyptians.' (v. 25)[2]

Nevertheless, the most persistent traditions of Yahweh as warrior link his activity, not with the Exodus, but with the traditions concerning the 'conquest' of the land of Canaan. Here, several elements need to be disentangled, even if their relation to each other and their relative dates are difficult to assess.

We note, first, the way that some traditions associate the Ark of the Covenant with battle and with one of Yahweh's titles, 'LORD of hosts'. Describing the march of the Israelites in their desert wanderings Numbers 10: 35f. says:

> And whenever the ark set out, Moses said, 'Arise, O LORD, and let thy enemies be scattered; and let them that hate thee flee before thee.' And when it rested, he said, 'Return, O LORD, to the ten thousand thousands of Israel.' (Nu. 10: 35f.)

I Samuel chapter 4 narrates an incident in battle when the Israelites sent for the Ark to be fetched from its place in the sanctuary to lead them out to battle, speaking of the Ark as the place where Yahweh was 'enthroned':

> So the people sent to Shiloh, and brought from there the ark of the covenant of the LORD of Hosts, who is enthroned on the cherubim . . . . (2 Sam. 4: 4)

The phrase 'LORD of Hosts' seems to equate Yahweh with the armies of Israel. Its frequent use in these early chapters of I Samuel where the scene is set at Shiloh where the Ark was said to be located, suggests again that the Ark was understood as a symbol of Yahweh's presence at the head of his armies. David's words to Goliath in I Samuel 17: 45 clearly link the title 'LORD of Hosts' with the armies of Israel:

> You come to me with a sword and a javelin; but I come to you in the name of the LORD of hosts, the God of the armies of Israel . . . .

Yet, sometimes, the 'hosts' are thought of as the 'hosts of heaven', the angelic powers who serve the purposes of God. So the prophet Micaiah sees a vision of God in heaven and says:

> I saw the LORD sitting on his throne, and all the host of heaven standing beside him on his right hand and on his left . . . . (I Ki. 22: 19)

When the enemy is menacing the Israelites in large numbers at Dothan, Elisha's servant is terrified. But Elisha prays:

> 'O LORD . . . open his eyes that he may see . . .' So the LORD opened the eyes of the young man . . . and, behold, the mountain was full of horses and chariots of fire . . . . (II Ki. 6: 17)

Further, Second Isaiah can refer to God as the creator of the stars and all the 'heavenly bodies':

> He who brings out their host by number,
> calling them all by name . . . . (Isa. 40: 26)

So, when Yahweh comes to fight for Israel against Sisera in the 'Song of Deborah' it is not surprising to read:

> From heaven fought the stars,
> from their courses they fought against Sisera. (Ju. 5: 20)

Again, even the sun takes part in the victory over the Amorites at Gibeon by 'standing still', so enabling Joshua to mount a night attack (Jos. 10: 6-14).

All this means that the 'LORD of Hosts' is the God of Israel's armies who has also at his command the heavenly angelic host and, as creator of heaven and earth, even the powers of the universe itself.

It is difficult to know how ancient this tradition of the part played by the Ark in warfare is. We hear the language of Numbers 10: 35f. in some of the Psalms, and the story of its role in the battle against the Philistines is only the opening prelude to a narrative whose climax is the taking up of the Ark to Jerusalem by David (I Sam. chs. 4-6, cf. II Sam. 6). This climax became the theme of cultic celebration in the Jerusalem temple. Ps. 132 gives us a dramatic re-presentation of the story told in II Samuel 6:

> Lo, we heard of it in Ephrathah,
> we found it in the fields of Ja'ar.
> Let us go to his dwelling place;
> let us worship at his footstool!
> Arise, O LORD, and go to thy resting place,
> thou and the ark of thy might. (Ps. 132: 6-8)

There, in a repetition of the words found in Numbers 10: 35f., we hear the cry which accompanied the carrying of the Ark into the temple. This is also associated with the divine choice of David and his line (vv. 11f.) and of Zion as his dwelling place (vv. 13-18).

We hear such a cultic cry again in a Psalm celebrating Yahweh's kingship:

> God has gone up with a shout,
> the LORD with the sound of a trumpet. (Ps. 47: 5)

This is to celebrate his victory over Israel's enemies:

> He subdued peoples under us,
> and nations under our feet. (v. 3)

The reference to the Ark in Shiloh spoke of it as a 'throne' for Yahweh. This was evidently its function in the Jerusalem temple, since a 'Deuteronomistic' passage[3] in the Book of Jeremiah, no doubt explaining the fact that the Ark was destroyed when the temple was razed to the ground in 586 BC, says:

> And when you have multiplied and increased in the land, in those days, says the LORD, they shall no more say, 'The ark of the covenant of the LORD'. It shall not come to mind, or be remembered, or missed . . . At that time *Jerusalem* shall be called the throne of the LORD [i.e. replacing the Ark]. (Jer. 3: 16f.)[4]

Another Psalm, Psalm 46, shows how the warrior tradition of 'Yahweh of Hosts' was taken over by the royal Zion theology:

> The nations rage, the kingdoms totter;
> he utters his voice, the earth melts.
> The LORD of hosts is with us;
> the God of Jacob is our refuge . . .
> He makes wars to cease to the end of the earth;
> he breaks the bow, and shatters the spear,
> he burns the chariot with fire! (Ps. 46: 6f., 9)

It is usually said that the ancient traditions of Yahweh as warrior of the pre-monarchical tribal confederacy were taken over and applied to the 'Zion theology' of royal court and temple attached to the Davidic dynasty in Jerusalem. This may be so, but it may also be that the Zion theology was projected back and so authenticated in such passages as Numbers 10: 35f. and I Samuel 4. We have no definitive method of dating the relevant material and so we cannot establish with certainty which came first.

The same applies to a second element in the Yahweh-warrior tradition, the 'coming forth' of God himself in war. At the beginning of this chapter we looked at 'The Song of the Sea' in Exodus chapter 15. Some scholars have pointed out how closely this echoes the Canaanite material describing the battle which Ba'al fought against Yam, the sea-god. Indeed, the parallels are so close, that such passages have been described as expressing the 'Divine Warrior' motif of the God who comes forth to do battle against the 'waters of chaos'. It may be remembered from an earlier chapter[5] that Ba'al's victory over the sea-god led to the building of a temple for him where he reigned as universal king. The Song of the Sea also leads up to the following claim:

> Terror and dread fell upon them;
> because of the greatness of thy arm, they are still as stone,
> till thy people, O LORD, pass by,
> till the people pass by whom thou hast purchased.
> Thou wilt bring them in, and plant them on thy own mountain,
> the place, O LORD, which thou hast made for thy abode,
> the sanctuary, LORD, which thy hands have established.
> The LORD will reign for ever and ever. (Exod. 15: 16-18)

The 'Divine Warrior' motif is heard also in the Song of Deborah:

> LORD, when thou didst go forth from Seir,
> when thou didst march from the region of Edom,
> the earth trembled,
> and the heavens dropped,
> yea, the clouds dropped water.
> The mountains quaked before the LORD,
> yon Sinai before the LORD, the God of Israel. (Ju. 5: 4f.)

The tradition that Yahweh marched forth as the Divine Warrior to secure victory over the enemies of his people is heard again in such a passage as Habakkuk 3: 3ff.:

> God came from Teman,
> and the Holy One from Mount Paran . . .
> His brightness was like the light,
> rays flashed from his hand;
> and there he veiled his power . . .
> Thou didst strip the sheath from thy bow,
> and put the arrows to the string . . .
> Thou didst crush the head of the wicked,
> laying him bare from thigh to neck. (Habk. 3: 3f., 9, 13)

The same tradition occur in some Psalms, for example, Ps. 68: 1, 7f.:

> Let God arise, let his enemies be scattered;
> let those who hate him flee before him! . . .
> O God, when thou didst go forth before thy people . . .
> the earth quaked at the presence of God;
> yon Sinai quaked at the presence of God.

In this Psalm we should notice how closely v. 4 echoes the Ugaritic description of Ba'al as 'the rider of the clouds', and how also the Psalm leads up to the idea of the presence of God in the sanctuary (v. 24).

The third element in the tradition of Yahweh as warrior is to be found in the concept of the 'holy war', associated with the conquest of Canaan. It is called 'holy war' because it was believed that the war was really God's war. Israel's enemies were his enemies and the Israelite armies were his instruments under his leadership. Regulations for the conduct of holy war are found in Deuteronomy chapter 20. The Israelites are instructed not to approach battle in fear because God is with them (v. 1), and this is to be proclaimed to the soldiers by a priest assuring them that it is God who fights for them (vv. 2-4). Those who have newly built a house as yet undedicated, or who have planted a vineyard which has not yet been harvested, or those who have recently married but whose marriage is as yet not consummated, are exempt from military service (vv. 5-7). Probably this originally had to do with securing rights of inheritance and succession, but, as Deuteronomy presents them, the regulations have a humanitarian basis. An opportunity is provided for the fearful to withdraw (vv. 8f.). Lack of faith in Yahweh's power to fight and win the battle was a great sin in the holy war theology and was strongly denounced by prophets when it resulted in the search for foreign allies to help out.

Rules for the conduct of war which follow are characteristically Deuteronomistic. The usual practice in war in the ancient world was to offer a city a chance to surrender. If it did not, all the men were slaughtered and the women, children and wealth of the city were taken as spoil. Deuteronomy, however, believed that all Canaanite cities and their inhabitants were to be wholly destroyed (7: 1ff.) and so it limits the more usual treatment to cities outside the area of Israel (vv. 10-15), while all others are to be 'put to the ban' (vv. 17-19). On the other hand, trees were not to be destroyed since they represent the long-term fruitfulness of the land (vv. 19f.).

The accounts of the conquest of the land in Joshua chapters 2-11 follow much of this. Before the entry, Joshua assures the people of God's presence and of his power to defeat the enemy. They are to 'sanctify themselves' (Jos. 3: 5). The Ark of the covenant is carried in front of them. Jericho falls miraculously by the mere cultic procession for seven days led by the Ark (Jos. 6) and, as a result, all its inhabitants (except Rahab and her family) and its possessions are directed to be put to the ban, i.e. totally destroyed. Nevertheless, sin in the holy community could result in the withdrawal of God's presence and so in their defeat. Because Achan sins by keeping some of the Canaanite possessions for himself (Jos. 7: 1) the whole Israelite army flees in defeat at Ai (vv. 2-5). Only when Achan and his family have themselves been 'put to the ban' (vv. 16-26), thus expiating the sin, do the Israelites see God's victory over the city (8: 1-29).

It is widely recognised that this account of the 'conquest' has been extremely schematised in Joshua 2-11 and that its present shape and form owe a great deal to Deuteronomic editors.[6] Some of the Deuteronomic literature, at least in its present form, is no earlier than the 7th. century BC, and the so-called 'Deuteronomistic History' was completed only during the exile. So we have no means of knowing how far this concept of holy war was an ideal construct, a purely theoretical element in the theology of the later Deuteronomists, or how far it really was part of the oldest tradition of the Israelite tribes. A few hints, however, point to its being, at least in some form, older than the 7th. century, and perhaps even older than the David-Zion cult in the Jerusalem of the monarchic period.

The first clue is that such ideas were widespread in the ancient Near East, and it is unlikely that Israel would not have shared them. For example, King Mesha, in the famous 'Moabite Stone' (9th. century BCE), inscribed words which attribute military defeat at the hand of the Israelite king, Omri, to the disapproval of his god, Chemosh.

> As for Omri, king of Israel, he humbled Moab many years, for Chemosh was angry at his land.[7]

Later, Chemosh again favoured him and directed him to fight a holy war:

> And Chemosh said to me, 'Go, take Nebo from Israel!'.

Later in the same inscription, victory at Jahaz is explicitly attributed to Chemosh:

> And the king of Israel had built Jahaz . . . but Chemosh drove him out before me.

Secondly, the fierce attacks by the prophets on any form of political or military alliances seem to stem from the idea of the holy war, as if such strategies undermine trust in Yahweh as warrior. This note is heard particularly in the teaching of Isaiah of Jerusalem:

> Woe to those who go down to Egypt for help
> and rely on horses,
> who trust in chariots because they are many
> and in horsemen because they are very strong,
> but do not look to the Holy One of Israel
> or consult the LORD! . . .
> The Egyptians are men and not God;
> their horses are flesh, and not spirit.
> When the LORD stretches out his hand,
> the helper will stumble, and he who is helped will fall,
> and they will all perish together. (Isa. 31: 1, 3)

Isaiah's call is for complete trust in God alone:

> In returning and rest you shall be saved;
> in quietness and in trust shall be your strength.
> And you would not, but you said,
> 'No! We will speed upon horses.' (Isa. 30: 15f.)

He illustrates this truth in his call to Ahaz to trust in God alone in face of the menace of the Syro-Ephraimite invasion:

> If you will not believe,

surely you shall not be established. (Isa. 7: 9)

If we heard that note only from Isaiah we might ascribe it to the influence of the 'Divine Warrior' motifs we heard in Psalms which celebrate the David-Zion theology. Yet we hear it also from a northern prophet like Hosea who is unlikely to have been influenced by those traditions. In Hosea chapter 14, part of the 'words' given for use by the penitent Israelites run:

> Assyria shall not save us,
> we will not ride upon horses . . . . (v. 3)

This follows the indictment of the prophet:

> When Ephraim saw his sickness,
> and Judah his wound,
> then Ephraim went to Assyria,
> and sent to the great king.
> But he is not able to cure you
> or heal your wound. (Hos. 5: 13)

Or again:

> Ephraim is like a dove,
> silly and without sense,
> calling to Egypt, going to Assyria. (Hos. 7: 11)

A third hint which suggests the antiquity of the holy war element in the tradition is supplied by another feature of the prophetic literature, namely the inclusion in most of the major prophetic collections of a section of oracles concerning foreign nations.[8] The issues of the date, authenticity, origin and process of tradition which lie behind each individual example of such oracles are complex, but the appearance of this type of oracle testifies to its place in the history of prophecy in Israel. The original function of the oracles was probably that of invective against national enemies, much as the old tradition records Balaam having been hired by the king of Moab to pronounce a curse against Israel in time of war (Nu. 22-24).

However, it is at this point that we should notice that, in the

GOD AS WARRIOR

hands of the pre-exilic prophets, the tradition of Yahweh as warrior takes a dramatic turn. Nowhere is this illustrated more forcefully than in the opening two chapters of Amos. Amos begins also with a series of oracles against foreign nations. They follow, in general, a schematised formula, each opening with the 'messenger formula', 'Thus says the LORD'. Next comes a 'numerical' saying characteristic of those in the Wisdom literature:

> For three transgressions of X
> and for four, I will not recall him [or 'it'].

The effect of the numerical sayings is to suggest an indefinite, but increasing, number of crimes on the part of those mentioned, Damascus, Gaza, Tyre, Edom, Ammon, Moab and Judah.[9] To this is added the details of the crime, all being those of excessive cruelty in time of war. Then follows the announcement of judgement in which 'fire' is seen as symbolic of invasion by foreign armies and destruction at the hand of invaders. No doubt Amos' Israelite hearers would have been cheered by such pronouncements of judgement against their neighbours and sometime enemies, and would have taken such oracles as being in the tradition of those against foreign nations to which they were accustomed. However, they were in for a shock. For, with exactly the same formula and in similar terms, suddenly Amos unleashes an oracle against Israel. This oracle, however, is longer than the others, and, whereas the other nations are charged with cruelty against their enemies, Israel is charged with cruelty against her own people:

> For three transgressions of Israel,
> and for four, I will not recall him. (Amos 2: 6)

The object of the verb to 'recall' is masculine. It may refer to 'judgement' generally, as most English Versions take it (RSV: 'I will not revoke the punishment'), or the 'him' may refer to the all too obvious threat in the mid-eighth century, the king of Assyria. Either way, the tradition is now being turned against Israel. The 'Day of Yahweh', which may refer either to his day of victory in battle or the 'Day' of the 'Enthronement Festival' when his victory over the cosmic forces of chaos was celebrated, is now a threat to Israel itself. It is a day of victory for Yahweh, the warrior, over his foes, but, by their conduct, the Israelites have made themselves his foes:

> Woe to you who desire the day of the LORD!
> Why would you have the day of the LORD?
> It is darkness, and not light. (Amos 5: 18)

This note recurs in the words of the pre-exilic and exilic prophets. Looking back on this period of Israel's history, a later prophet can say (Isa. 63: 9bf.):

> ... in his love and in his pity he redeemed them;
> he lifted them up and carried them
> all the days of old.
> But they rebelled
> and grieved his holy Spirit;
> therefore he turned to be their enemy,
> and himself fought against them.

Jeremiah brought God's word to Zedekiah:

> I myself will fight against you with outstretched hand and strong arm, in anger, and in fury, and in great wrath. (Jer. 21: 5)

Here the very 'Deuteronomistic' vocabulary of their salvation history is used. This often spoke of God bringing Israel out of Egypt with 'an outstretched hand and a strong arm' (e.g. Deut. 26: 8). Yet such language is now turned against his own people. Salvation history will become judgement history.

This leads us to another application of the 'Divine Warrior' motif in the Old Testament. It occurs in the more sharply eschatological passages in later prophecy which look forward to the end time when God will intervene in world history, bringing the present dominance of the evil powers to an end and ushering in his own rule as king. The use of the creation myth which characterised the Zion liturgy, and the recollection of Yahweh's great interventions in Israel's history, together became a paradigm for a final and complete victory over all that represented 'chaos'. So the last chapter in Zechariah looks forward to Yahweh's day of battle against the oppressor nations which threaten Jerusalem:

> Then the LORD will go forth and fight against those nations as when he fights on a day of battle . . . Then the LORD your God will come, and all the holy ones with him . . . And the LORD will become king over all the earth . . .' (Zech. 14: 3, 5b, 9a)

Another oracle depicts the terror which will seize the nations as they come:

> Hark, a tumult on the mountains
> as of a great multitude!
> Hark, an uproar of the kingdoms
> of nations gathering together! . . .
> Wail, for the day of the LORD is near;
> as destruction from the Almighty it will come! . . .
> Behold, the day of the LORD comes,
> cruel, with wrath and fierce anger,
> to make the earth a desolation
> and to destroy its sinners from it. (Isa. 13: 4, 6, 9)

This occurs in an oracle against Babylon, but it is clearly late and one in which 'Babylon' has become a 'type' of all enemies of Yahweh's purposes for universal peace. It is a note which runs through much late prophetic literature. One more example must suffice:

> For behold, the LORD will come in fire,
> and his chariots like the storm-wind,
> to render his anger in fury,
> and his rebuke with flames of fire.
> For by fire will the LORD execute judgement,
> and by his sword, upon all flesh;
> and those slain by the LORD shall be many. (Isa. 66: 15)

Strangely, such passages can occur close to others which are more 'universalist' in spirit. Isaiah chapter 66 itself includes the words,

> For as the new heavens and the new earth
> which I will make
> shall remain before me, says the LORD;
> so shall your descendants and your name remain.
> From new moon to new moon,
> and from sabbath to sabbath,
> all flesh shall come to worship before me,
> says the LORD. (Isa. 66: 22f.)

Again, Zechariah chapter 14 ends with a fine vision of all nations coming to worship Yahweh at Jerusalem:

> Then every one that survives of all the nations that have come against Jerusalem shall go up year after year to worship the King, the LORD of hosts. (Zech. 14: 16)

It is as though, on the one hand, Yahweh the divine warrior strikes down all evil and its representatives, in order that on the other hand not Israel alone, but all nations shall live under his reign as universal and everlasting King. That is how the earth will once more know peace. Nowhere is this more finely expressed than in an oracle common both to Isaiah and to Micah:

> It shall come to pass in the latter days
> that the mountain of the house of the LORD
> shall be established as the highest of the mountains,
> and shall be raised above the hills;
> and all the nations shall flow to it.
> And many peoples shall come, and say,
> 'Come let us go up to the mountain of the LORD,
> to the house of the God of Jacob;
> that he may teach us his ways
> and that we may walk in his paths' . . .
> He shall judge between the nations,
> and shall decide for many peoples;
> and they shall beat their swords into plowshares,
> and their spears into pruning hooks;
> nation shall not lift up sword against nation,
> neither shall they learn war any more. (Isa. 2: 2-4 = Mic. 4: 1-4)

Yahweh may be the 'Divine Warrior', but he is no arbitrary champion of one nation, determined to serve its interests alone in striking at their enemies. Some prophets, at least, see that he is the warrior who contests evil in all its forms and wherever it occurs. His own people will know no immunity if they, too, identify themselves with that evil. The ultimate aim of the warrior God is not domination by one privileged nation, but a universal peace where all nations live together in harmony and peace, because all alike live in subjection to the righteous will of him who is universal king.

NOTES TO CHAPTER EIGHT

1. The Hebrew phrase *yām sûph*, usually translated 'Red Sea' actually means 'Sea of Reeds'.

2. This passage is usually assigned to the 'Yahwistic' source of the Pentateuch: see chapter 2, n. 1 above.

3. See chapter 2, n. 2 above.

4. It is interesting that in the 'Deuteronomistic' traditions, the Ark tends to be 'demythologised'. In Deut. ch. 10, the Ark is neither a portable war shrine, nor a 'throne' for Yahweh in the temple, but simply a box which contains the tables of the law (Deut. 10: 1-9).

5. See above, pp. 110f.

6. The difficulties involved in attempting to reconstruct the 'actual history' of the settlement of the Israelite tribes in Canaan are probably impenetrable. This is due partly to the nature of the Old Testament material which is concerned more with the theological interpretation of the traditions than the presentation of 'historical fact', and partly because the evidence from archaeology is still ambiguous. A useful survey of various attempts to deal with these problems is offered by M. Weippert, *The Settlement of the Israelite Tribes in Palestine*, Studies in Biblical Theology, 2nd. Series, No. 21, London, 1971. A more recent survey, which is critical of some aspects of Weippert's work, is to be found in N.P. Lemche, *Early Israel: Anthropological and Historical*

Studies on the Israelite Society Before the Monarchy, Supplements to Vetus Testamentum, XXXVII, Leiden, 1985.

7. The translation of the text here and in the following quotations from the Moabite Stone are to be found in J.B. Pritchard (ed.), *Ancient Near Eastern Texts* (see ch. 3 n.4), p. 320.

8. The main collections of such oracles are Isa. chs. 13-23, Jer. chs. 46-51, Ezek. chs. 25-32.

9. The oracle against Judah is undoubtedly later, coming from a time when the Book of Amos was edited in the South after the fall of the Northern Kingdom of Israel. A number of commentators also believe that the oracles against Edom and Tyre are later additions. The issue of the date of these particular oracles does not affect the point being made here.

IX

GOD AS LOVER

Perhaps the most unexpected and even daring of the human pictures of God used in the Old Testament is that of God as 'Lover'. To use language drawn from human sexuality to describe him and his relationship with his people seems totally unexpected when, as we have seen,[1] any suggestion of a relationship between Yahweh and a female consort was officially taboo, and cults which involved sexual rites were so strongly forbidden. Yet Hosea, the prophet who appears to initiate the use of such language (although of course we do not know how far he was drawing on traditions now lost to us), combines to a unique degree sexual language about Yahweh with fierce denunciation of Canaanite fertility cults and practices.

To understand the force behind both the symbolic language and the denunciations, it is necessary to grasp something of the nature of a fertility religion like that of the Canaanites. It was the religion of an essentially agricultural society for which the coming of the rain to make the earth fertile was essential to life. Today, to control the earth and make it yield produce, farmers take chemical analyses of the soil to determine which nutrients it needs and provide water by irrigation or some other means. At that time, however, the lifegiving property of the soil was a mystery akin to that of a woman bearing a child in her womb. Rain was like male semen penetrating the womb of the earth to make it fertile. Both were divine gifts and divine activities and the way to ensure the 'sacral marriage' between the god and the earth was to control it through the proper manipulation of the cult. A feature of Canaanite religion was the attachment to the sanctuaries of male and female cult prostitutes. Their procreative rites were believed, like acts of 'sympathetic' or 'mimetic' magic, to ensure the necessary procreative activity of the god Ba'al, in whose hands was the power to give rain and so consummate the sacral marriage with the soil.

All this is closely connected with the religious epics which feature the activities of Ba'al in the Canaanite literature. In these, Ba'al is defeated in battle by the god 'Môt' (= 'death') and descends to the underworld. Before he does so, however, he copulates with a heifer (the goddess Anat) and so his last act ensures the future fertility of the earth. Ba'al's time in the underworld corresponds to the dry, summer period. Eventually, however, Anat secures Ba'al's release from the realm of death by slaying Môt. As Ba'al 'rises from the dead', the winter rains come to make the earth fertile again.

Clearly this is one form of the myth of the 'dying and rising god' so widespread through the ancient world, a myth associated with the cycle of the seasons and with the life and death of vegetation in summer and winter. It is evident that the cult was widely practised in the land of Canaan in Israelite times. This is not only because the Israelites were attracted by it when they came into the settled land from the desert, as has been so often argued. From the time of David onwards, when the old Canaanite city states were absorbed into the monarchic state and what had now become the 'nation' of Israel, there was a large proportion of the population for whom this was their traditional religion anyway. It is easy to understand why it should spread to the Israelites, who, for the most part, simply added the worship of Ba'al to that of Yahweh or identified the two. Yahweh was a desert and nomadic God, perhaps most of all, as we have seen, a war God. To assure a good crop from the soil it would seem necessary to enlist the help of Ba'al. It was his land and he was the god of fertility.

Just how widespread the cult of Ba'al became is clear from the number of personal names with Ba'al compounds in them. (A later editor went through the Books of Samuel changing all the Ba'al elements into 'bosheth', the Hebrew word for 'shame'. Thus the name of Saul's son was not actually 'Ishbosheth' but

'Ishba'al'). Again, we have references to Canaanite religious practices. For example, Gideon's father had an altar to Ba'al (Ju. 6: 25) and Elijah's conflict with the four hundred and fifty prophets of Ba'al on Mount Carmel testifies to the popularity of the cult, even if some of this was due to a deliberate campaign by the foreign Jezebel to make it the official cult of Israel. Finally, the frequent attacks of the prophets and the Deuteronomists offer their own testimony. Prophets do not waste their time attacking practices that do not happen.

This is the background to Hosea's preaching as a prophet. At one time it was customary for scholars to claim that we know a good deal about his personal life which, they believed, was intimately related to his message. Nowadays, most commentators are justifiably more cautious. Any information we have of the prophet's personal life is presumably to be found in chapters 1 and 3 of the book. The wide variety of interpretations of the material the older commentators confidently offered, however, would alone counsel caution. Some thought chapter 3 was a sequel to the story of his marriage related in chapter 1. A favourite reconstruction of this was that Gomer, the wife he is there said to have married, proved unfaithful to him, so that Hosea had later to buy her back from some unspecified servitude. There is, however, very little in chapter 1 to suggest that Gomer was unfaithful. Others thought the two chapters represented parallel, but independent accounts of the same marriage. The great differences between them made this difficult to sustain, however. Others thought that they represented two distinct incidents involving different women. Others, again, thought the whole thing was an allegory of Israel's relation as a wife to her husband, Yahweh.

The fact is that the two chapters do not tell us enough to be sure, nor is it easy to determine exactly what 'genre' of prophetic literature they belong to. It is uncertain whether we should read them as connected narrative at all. Chapter 1 is about Hosea's marriage, told by someone else and narrated in the third person. God commands him to take a 'wife of harlotry' and have 'children of harlotry', for the land has committed great harlotry in forsaking Yahweh. He marries Gomer, the daughter of Diblaim (the lack of any symbolic meaning to the names suggests we are dealing with actual narrative rather than allegory). Hosea has three children by her, two sons and a daughter. Only of the first is it said explicitly that Gomer bore him 'to Hosea', but this is a slender basis on which to rear whole romantic novels of Gomer's unfaithfulness. Each of the three children is given a name symbolic of God's coming judgement on Israel. The first is called 'Jezreel', indicating that God would avenge the bloody purge of Jehu against the house of Omri in the Valley of Jezreel a century earlier (II Ki. 9: 1-28, 10: 1-14). This action, according to tradition, had been sanctioned by an earlier prophet, Elijah (cf. I Ki. 19: 17). The two other names, 'Not-pitied' and 'Not my people' suggest God's rejection of his covenant relationship with Israel. Later additions to the chapter are found in v. 7 which contrasts God's attitude to Judah with that of his rejection of Israel, and vv. 10f. which announce the future reversal of the judgement just threatened by the names of the children. In 3: 1-4 we find first person narrative, apparently by Hosea himself. Either 'God says to him again' or God says, 'Go again' (the Hebrew could yield either meaning) and commands him to love a woman already loved by another man and an adulteress. The word 'man' means just 'companion' or 'associate', but the context, in which she is called an 'adulteress', and the use of the word in the plural in a similar context in Jeremiah 3: 1 ('You have played the harlot with many *lovers*') suggests that this is an illicit relationship. The word for 'companion' is very similar to the word for 'evil' and the LXX (Septuagint) and Syriac versions read 'a woman *loving evil*'. The parallel is drawn, however, with God's love for Israel even though the people turn to other gods and their worship. Hosea therefore 'buys' this woman from some apparently forced service for fifteen shekels of silver and a lethech of barley. Why that particular sum is mentioned is not clear. In the law a slave was valued at thirty shekels (Exod. 21: 32) and, in Leviticus 27: 4, the value of a female who had taken a vow was also thirty shekels. That was the cost for commuting the vow. This has led some to suggest that this woman had either been sold into slavery or had taken a vow in the service of some god at a sanctuary, perhaps as a cult prostitute. This, however, is not made explicit.

Hosea makes her live as his 'for many days'. She is not to have relations with any other man and, he says, 'So will I also be to you'. This is also seen as symbolic of the fact that God will chasten his people by taking them away from all the temptations of their present settled life in the land. They will again live in the desert without king or any of the apparatus of the worship involved in alien cults. A later addition (v. 5) looks beyond this to a return to the land under the rule of a Davidic king.

The passage abounds in obscurities. We are not told the name of the woman, nor why Hosea has to buy her. There is no mention of the children in this chapter, nothing to say that this is Gomer at all. It is not clear what the Hebrew of the second part of v. 3 means. Literally it reads, 'You shall not be for (or belong to) a man (LXX adds 'another' man) and (or 'but') I moreover to you.' Often that is taken to mean, 'You shall have no sexual relations with any men and I will avoid all sexual relations with you'. But it could equally mean, 'and I also will remain faithful to you'. Nor are we told the outcome of Hosea's action except in v. 5, which is probably either a later addition as a whole from the time of the exile, or one in which just the reference to David as king is later. Certainly the northern Israelites would not have cared about being under a Davidic king again, but Hosea may have seen a return after this period of discipleship and trial, and the reference to the king may have been added to this more general prediction.

With so much uncertainty it would be a rash commentator who claimed to have the definitive interpretation. Perhaps the most we can say is that we appear to have *two acts of 'prophetic symbolism'* here. 'Prophetic symbolism' is the name for the deeds which a prophet would perform in addition to the spoken words of his oracles. Both words and deeds were, they believed, commissioned by Yahweh. Both were 'words', the Hebrew word *dābār* standing for word and deed, in one case the word being visual and in the other oral. Both it was believed shared the efficacy which not only announced Yahweh's intentions but set in motion the power which effected those intentions. First, the marriage with Gomer symbolised God's intentions to judge a people who had acted like 'harlots' in their faithlessness in deserting Yahweh for another god. Second, the action with the woman described in chapter 3, whoever the woman was, also symbolised God's intention to judge his people. However, this appears to have spoken also of a continuing purpose of God towards his people, of his intention, after a period of discipline, to bring them back to a single-minded, faithful relationship with him.

This would fit in with the general sense of the oracles which occur in chapter 2 which use the metaphor of God as 'husband' to Israel. Individual Israelites, like the children of a marriage, are urged to plead with their mother (Israel) to give up her adultery. She has forsaken her husband (Yahweh) for relations with other lovers (the Canaanite gods). So he intends to make her way hard to the point where she cries out,

> 'I will return to my first husband,
> for it was better with me then than now.' (Hos. 2: 7b)

It was absurd for Israel to have forsaken Yahweh for the fertility cult of Ba'al, because it was Yahweh who was the true fertility God:

> And she did not know
> that it was I who gave her
> the grain, the wine and the oil,
> and who lavished upon her silver and gold
> which they used for Ba'al. (v. 8)

God will therefore judge her by taking all the produce of the land away and preventing her access to the fertility cults of Ba'al. He will drive her out of the land into the wilderness. That, however, is not to be the end of the story. God will go with her into the desert in order to win her back. The language here is explicitly sexual.

> Therefore, behold, I will *entice* her . . . . (2: 14)

It is a striking verb to put into God's mouth. In Exodus 22: 16 we read in the law relating to the seduction of an unbetrothed virgin:

> If a man *seduces* [the same word Hosea uses of God] a virgin who is not betrothed, and lies with her, he shall give the marriage present for her, and make her his wife.

Or we read of the instructions to Delilah given by the Philistines regarding her husband, Samson:

> *Entice* your husband to tell us what the riddle is . . . . (Ju. 14: 15)

And again:

> And the lords of the Philistines came to her and said to her, '*Entice* him, and see wherein his great strength lies . . . .' (Ju. 16: 5)

Of the use of the verb in Hosea one commentator has said, 'Like a lover who plots to be alone with his beloved, Yahweh will take the beloved into the wilderness.'[2] This sexual enticement will be successful:

> And in that day, says the LORD, you will call me, 'My husband,' and no longer will you call me, 'My Ba'al.' (2: 16)

There is a play on words in that sentence since in Hebrew the word 'Ba'al' can also mean 'husband' (e.g. Gen. 20: 3, Exod. 21: 3, 22). Finally, Yahweh's courtship will lead to a renewed covenant relationship. The judgement threatened in the names of the children will be reversed and the people will be called once more 'Pitied' and 'My People' (vv. 21-23).

Frequently in the book Israel's participation in the Ba'al cults is likened to adultery and prostitution.

> My people inquire of a thing of wood,
> and their staff gives them oracles.
> For a spirit of harlotry has led them astray,
> and they have left their God to play the harlot.
> They sacrifice on the tops of the mountains,
> and make offerings upon the hills,
> under oak, poplar, and terebinth,
> because their shade is good. (4: 12-14)

Or again:

> Rejoice not O Israel!
> Exult not like the peoples;
> for you have played the harlot,
> forsaking your God.
> You have loved a harlot's hire
> upon all threshing floors. (9: 1)

Hosea does a very dangerous thing in using this picture. This is not simply because of his use of sexual language as an image of God's relation with Israel. He takes over the very language of the 'sacral marriage' of the Ba'al cult, the central feature of the religious practices he is attacking. It is as though he were saying, 'All you are looking for in Ba'al and his worship is to be found in Yahweh'. The significant shift in his use of the 'sacral marriage' concept, however, is that Yahweh has no sexual relation with any female consort. Nor, for all that he is the true God of fertility, is the marriage with the land. Yahweh loves his people Israel as a husband loves his bride. The covenant is like a marriage contract between them. However, where the law allowed divorce for infidelity in marriage (Deut. 24: 1), Yahweh remains faithful to his love, seeking to win back his faithless partner. Perhaps it is no coincidence that a prominent word in Hosea's prophecy is the word *hesed*. That is basically a legal term and means faithfulness to the terms of a legal contract. Since God goes on showing such fidelity far beyond the requirements of the law, it comes to have the overtone of 'grace', the undeserved devotion and loyalty of a persistent love.

Some form of the word *hesed* occurs no fewer than six times in the book. The best known is in 6: 6:

> For I desire *hesed* and not sacrifice,
> the knowledge of God, rather than burnt offerings.

Such a quality will be possible, because Yahweh promises

> And I will betroth you to me for ever; I will betroth you to me
> in righteousness and in justice, in *hesed*, and in mercy. (2: 19)

Hosea's use of the picture of the relationship between Yahweh and Israel as that of lover and betrothed was an influential one.

Jeremiah takes it up and uses it in very similar terms. Like Hosea, he sees Israel as once in the desert having had a 'honeymoon' period with Yahweh when she was faithful to him before she succumbed, in the land of Canaan, to the temptations of other cults.

> I remember the devotion of your youth,
> your love as a bride,
> how you followed me in the wilderness,
> in a land not sown. (Jer. 2: 2)

By contrast now:

> If a man divorces his wife
> and she goes from him,
> and becomes another man's wife,
> will he return to her? . . .
> You have played the harlot with many lovers;
> and would you return to me? says the LORD . . .
> By the wayside you have sat awaiting lovers
> like an Arab in the wilderness.
> You have polluted the land
> with your vile harlotry.
> Therefore the showers have been withheld,
> and the spring rain has not come;
> you have a harlot's brow,
> yet you refuse to be ashamed. (Jer. 3: 1-3)

Or again:

> Can a maiden forget her ornaments,
> or a bride her attire?
> Yet my people have forgotten me
> days without number. (2: 32)

Ezekiel develops the picture in a distinctive way, distinctive both in literary form by means of extended allegory, and in his use of language which becomes both more explicitly sexual and more coarse. In chapter 16 the prophet tells the story of the foundling girl, taken care of by a prince and eventually married by him when she grew up to womanhood. However she uses the wealth and position he gives her to have relations with many other men. Accordingly she will be judged. It is an allegory of Yahweh's relation with Israel, personified as 'Jerusalem', whom he found as a 'baby' in Egypt. A closely related message is found in chapter 23 which tells the story of two sisters, Oholah and Oholibah. In the allegory they represent the two kingdoms of Israel and Judah. The difference from Hosea and Jeremiah is that, for Ezekiel, they played the harlot from the very beginning of their history in Egypt. There was no 'honeymoon' period before their entry into Canaan. The coarse language is, no doubt, a literary device to express the prophet's revulsion and horror at the sins of Israel. The foundling girl was discovered without navel cord cut, unwashed, weltering in the blood of birth, while the nation's continuing faithlessness is described in the most explicit language of prostitution and sexual immorality.

No doubt, all this must be seen against the background of God's 'jealousy' for his people, for jealousy is part of human sexuality, born of the desire to possess the one loved. So there is a law relating to the jealous husband in Numbers 5: 11-31 and his authority to submit a wife he suspects of unfaithfulness to what we should call a 'trial by ordeal'. Inexplicable and repulsive as it all seems to us, the point in mentioning it here is to note the Hebrew word for 'jealousy' (*qîn'ah*) with its related verb, 'to be jealous' (*qānā'*).

> If a spirit of jealousy comes upon him, and he is jealous of his wife who has defiled herself . . . . (v. 14)

(or even if he merely suspects her and she is not, in fact, guilty) then he may bring her for trial. This is exactly the emotion felt by Yahweh, Israel's husband, towards his unfaithful bride:

> and they shall know that I, the LORD, have spoken in *jealousy*, when I spend my fury upon them . . . . (Ezek. 5: 13)

The same word occurs in Ezekiel chapter 23 in the allegory of Oholah and Oholibah:

> I will direct my *jealousy* against you, that they may deal with you in fury . . . . (23: 25)

GOD AS LOVER

This stems from the Decalogue in which worship of other gods was forbidden because, 'I the LORD your God am a jealous God . . . .'

Nevertheless, Hosea's use of the picture of God as lover to portray a love in God which will not finally let his bride go but will persist in grace and win her back for all her impurity, is not lost in the Old Testament. In the later chapters of the Book of Isaiah, the desolate, mourning, lonely Zion is to know again the joy of betrothal:

> I will greatly rejoice in the LORD,
> my soul shall exult in my God;
> for he has clothed me in garments of salvation,
> he has covered me with the robe of righteousness,
> as a bridegroom decks himself with a garland,
> and as a bride adorns herself with her jewels. (Isa. 61: 10)

It is not exactly clear who the speaker is. Quite possibly it is Zion, who is the object of the prophet's ministry as stated in v. 3, '. . . to grant to those who mourn in Zion . . .'. This will, then, be the song of praise of those who before uttered the lament of despair to God, but who now rejoice in his salvation.

In Isaiah 62: 5 Zion is addressed with a promise. As so often, words in these latest chapters of the book echo words of Second Isaiah (chs. 40-55). Second Isaiah had promised that the community which felt that God had forsaken them will yet see all her exiled people returning. They will be like bridal ornaments at her wedding ceremony:

> Lift up your eyes round about and see;
> they all gather, as they come to you.
> As I live, says the LORD,
> you shall put them all on as an ornament,
> you shall bind them on as a bride does. (Isa. 49: 18)

So the wife who had said,

> I was bereaved and barren,
> exiled and put away . . . . (v. 21)

will now find herself a bride and 'mother' again. This is the theme taken up by the later prophet following the return:

> You shall no more be termed 'Forsaken',
> and your land shall no more be called 'Desolate';
> but you shall be called 'My delight is in her' [Heb. *Hephzibah*]
> and your land 'Married' [Heb. *Be'ûlah*];
> for the LORD delights in you,
> and your land shall be married.
> For as a young man marries a virgin,
> so shall your sons marry you,
> and as the bridegroom rejoices over the bride,
> so shall your God rejoice over you. (Isa. 62: 4f.)

'Your land married'. The Hebrew word is a form of the term *Ba'al*, *Be'ûlah* being the passive participle of the related verb. With its nuance of 'husband' we have returned to the idea of the sacral marriage by which the god makes the soil fertile. But if this leans towards the Canaanite concept of the god who is related to the *land*, what follows soon reverts to the idea of Yahweh as married to the *community* of Zion. The Hebrew text which speaks of 'your sons marrying you' (v. 5) gives little sense. However, the slightest emendation would give us the sense, 'Your *builder* (i.e. Yahweh) shall marry you', and this is the reading which has been followed by NEB and JB.

So Zion, once forsaken and bereaved, is to know again the joyful scene of a wedding, restored as the 'bride' of Yahweh. It is not a very far step from this climax to the Old Testament picture of God as the triumphant 'Lover' whose love triumphs over all the sin and rejection of his beloved, to the vision of the 'New Jerusalem' of St. John in the New Testament:

> And I saw the holy city, new Jerusalem, coming down out of heaven from God, prepared as a bride adorned for her husband. (Rev. 21: 2)

The Old Testament picture, then, is a rich one. Yahweh, as 'Lover', takes the initiative in wooing and winning his people as his 'bride'. He loves them with a love which refuses to give them up, outsoaring the requirements of law on the wings of grace.

Such love is the ultimate source of hope throughout the failure and suffering of his people. It has its own power to make the unworthy worthy and, at the end, it will triumph over all obstacles. The last word in heaven and on earth is with the triumph of God, the Lover.

NOTES TO CHAPTER NINE

1. See above in ch. 3, p. 71, and below, p. 209.

2. J.L. Mays, *Hosea*, SCM Press, Old Testament Library, London, 1969.

X

GOD AS FEMININE

There can be no arguing with the fact that Yahweh, the God of the Old Testament, appears as very much a male figure. We have seen him to possess the predominantly male characteristics of fatherhood, strength, kingship, of the male kinsman who acts as 'redeemer', and of 'warrior'. Even as lover, he is the male lover who woos and betrothes his bride. Personal pronouns relating to God are masculine, not least in the solemn assertion found often in Second Isaiah and elsewhere where God says 'I am *He*' (e.g. Isa. 41: 4, 42: 8, 43: 10, etc.). While this can virtually be translated as 'I am God', the fact remains that the pronoun is masculine.

We may applaud or abhor all this. We cannot pretend it is otherwise. While every generation will, and must, read an ancient text in the context of its own cultural life and mores, we cannot baptize the substance of the text into the spirit of our own time if that means forcing it to say something it neither intended nor carried as an 'undertone' beneath the level of its conscious meaning.

Nevertheless, it is a legitimate question to ask, 'As well as the explicit masculinity of Yahweh in the Old Testament is there any implicit "femininity"?' The predominant picture is of Yahweh as male. Is that the whole picture, however? A number of feminist scholars and writers have suggested that it is not.[1] In this final study it is our intention to hunt for clues to the 'feminine' picture of God.

Our starting point must be the first chapter of Genesis:

So God created man [Heb. *'ādām* = 'humankind'] in his own image; male and female he created them. (Gen. 1: 27)

A very great deal has been written, and continues to be written, about this trenchant, but somewhat enigmatic phrase. What does it mean to say that human beings are created 'in the image of God?' Any discussion must take note of the word 'image' (Heb. *tselem*) which is often used of the 'images' of other gods, and so prohibited to Yahwism. It is most often therefore used in pejorative terms. Nevertheless, it implies that, what 'images' are to other gods, human beings are to Yahweh. Discussion must take notice of the fact that this term is used in parallelism to the word 'likeness' (Heb. *dᵉmûth*) and of its repetition in Genesis 5: 1f., again in the context of *'ādām* being created by God 'male and female'. It must consider the use of both terms in Genesis 5: 3 of Adam's own son, Seth, for that implies that there is some analogy between the relation of children to their parents and human beings to God. It must not miss the re-use of the phrase 'image of God' in the Priestly Writer's description of the covenant made between God and Noah after the flood (Gen. 9: 1-17, see especially v. 6). So much of Genesis chapter 1 is repeated in these verses–the drying up of the waters of chaos, the command to 'be fruitful and multiply', the reference to the plants and animals, the place of human beings as 'in the image of God' and their task as God's vicegerent. There is a new creation after the flood.

Indeed, for many, it is the role assigned to humankind as a kind of sub-creator which is at the heart of what it means to say that people are made in God's image. A proper discussion of the term must also give due weight to the many points of contact seen between people and God in the Old Testament, some of which have been the theme of these studies. Nevertheless, it must not forget the differences stressed between God and even the highest of his creatures, he 'spirit', they 'flesh'. On the other hand it must remember what is said of human beings in Psalm 8 which offers a kind of commentary on Genesis 1. All of these issues, and more, are properly the field of investigation into the meaning of the phrase 'image of God' when applied to humankind. We must certainly also examine the comparative material of the Ancient Near East. Even so, its exact nuances remain elusive. Caution must wait on all our attempts at definition and explanation. As with much poetic symbol, the truth it conveys may well be bigger than our neat mental concepts. Yet it is strange how often the discussion appears one-sided. We rifle the metaphor for light it may throw on human nature. Much less frequently do we ask what light it may throw on the divine nature. If God, in creating humankind male and female so that humanity is made up of two complementary, inter-dependent qualities (whatever be the exact qualities we mean by 'male' and 'female'), so created them in his own image, may it not be inferred that these two qualities co-exist somehow in him?

This is the more likely, one is almost tempted to say 'necessary', since, certainly for the Priestly Writer as for much 'official' Old Testament theology, God is one. There is no other. There may be hints in Genesis chapter 1 of the influence of the Babylonian creation epic *Enuma Elish*. In both, the pre-existing state of the cosmos was a dark, formless watery 'chaos' ocean. As *Tiamat* was the dragon monster symbolising these waters in the Babylonian story, so, in Hebrew, these waters are referred to as *tehôm*, the 'deep'. The two words are almost certainly related etymologically. But, that said, the great difference is that, in the Genesis account, there is no pantheon with one god championing the rest. There is no conflict between two powers of almost equal strength like Marduk and Tiamat. One God acts alone in sovereign power creating all by his divine word. Even if the interesting 'Let us make man in our image' does refer to other divine beings, these have long since been subordinated to the role of angelic messengers who run Yahweh's errands and who, under his control, form the 'Council of Heaven'. Denied any kind of female consort it would not be surprising if Yahweh had been thought of as comprising within himself both male and female qualities.

We have already examined one area where this indeed proved to be so. God, the creator, combined both male and female roles in procreation. We saw in our study of 'God as Father', that the Hebrew verb 'to beget' can be used of both the male and female parts in conception and birth. The verb is used for both in Zechariah 13: 3:

> And if any one appears as a prophet, his father and mother who bore him [plural participle of the verb *yāladh*] will say to him, 'You shall not live.'

On one occurrence, indeed, the specifically female part in birth is used of Yahweh:

> 'You were unmindful of the Rock that begot you, and you forgot the God who *gave you birth* [Heb. *ḥûl*].' (Deut. 32: 18)

The second verb (*ḥûl*) means basically, 'to whirl', 'dance' or 'writhe', and hence its application to the process of birth, the birth-pangs or spasms of the mother as she delivers the child.[2]

It is used also of Yahweh 'bringing forth' the earth.

> Before the mountains *were brought forth* [Heb. *ḥûl*] or ever thou hadst formed the earth and the world, from everlasting to everlasting, thou art God. (Ps. 90: 2)

In our study of God as 'father', we noted that little is made in the Old Testament, especially when compared with other ancient Near Eastern literature, of the fact that God is 'father' to *all* peoples by virtue of his act of creation. Instead the emphasis is on the truth that he '*begot*' Israel by delivering them from bondage in Egypt. We suggested that this may have been due partly to the desire to avoid any implication that, in the act of creation, Yahweh took part in any sexual activity with a female consort. This distinguished Yahweh from the gods of fertility cults like Ba'al. It underlined the fact that there was only one God of Israel who had, therefore, to combine the two roles within himself.

At this point in our discussion it is well to admit that it is extremely difficult to talk about male and female 'qualities'. It would be facile to take certain human characteristics such as aggression, power, assertiveness, anger, initiative, and dub them 'male'. It is equally over-simple to take qualities like gentleness, receptivity, kindliness, passivity, and dub them 'female'. Not only are such qualities abstract in themselves and very difficult to define, and such stereotyping of images may itself be the product of a male-dominated culture, but the fact is that they co-exist to a greater or lesser degree in all human beings. Perhaps we should be thinking of a male and female 'way' of combining or expressing all these characteristics, rather than assigning them to specific genders, but even so there is something of the 'male' and 'female' in us all. Any of these qualities may be more prominent, or even slightly out of balance, in some people more than others, be they male or female. We must be on our guard, therefore, against starting with the fixed idea that certain qualities, when they are assigned to Yahweh in the Old Testament, testify to the masculine or feminine in the deity. We must seek, as far as we can, for greater objectivity.

We might start from the observable fact that the Old Testament does move towards giving a high place to women in the family, in society and in religion. Nothing alters the fact that it was basically a patriarchal, or as we should say, a male-dominated society. There is, however, a move in law, for example, to grow beyond the position that a wife is the mere possession of her husband with no legal rights of her own. So Deuteronomy is the first law-code to grant women legal rights as citizens before the law. The commandment in Exodus 20: 17 reads,

> You shall not covet your neighbour's house; you shall not covet your neighbour's wife, or his manservant, or his maidservant, or his ox, or his ass, or anything that is your neighbour's.

In Deuteronomy there is an important change:

> Neither shall you covet your neighbour's wife; and you shall not desire your neighbour's house, his field, or his manservant, or his maidservant, his ox, or his ass, or anything that is your neighbour's. (Deut. 5: 21)

It may seem a small concession to the dignity of women to put their value above that of a house, but at least it must be seen as a step in the right direction!

In Deuteronomy 12: 12 (cf. v. 18) the law is extended to relate to a daughter and to a maidservant:

> 'And you shall rejoice before the LORD your God, you and your sons and your daughters, your menservants and your maidservants . . . .'

Or, again, in Deuteronomy 29: 10f.

> You shall stand this day all of you before the LORD your God; the heads of your tribes, your elders, and your
> officers, all the men of Israel, your little ones, your wives, and the sojourner who is in your camp . . . .

In Exodus 34: 16 Israelites were forbidden to intermarry with Canaanite women. In Deuteronomy 7: 3 this is extended to Israelite women as well. They are not to intermarry with Canaanite men. Later on, the law of inheritance appears to have been extended to daughters. Numbers 27: 1-11 tells the story of the daughters of Zelophehad who approached Moses and the priests and leaders of the congregation after the death of their father. He had no son, only daughters and, by existing law, the land would have passed to his brothers. In the form of a new word of God to Moses, the former ruling is overturned and the daughters in such cases are granted right of succession. This occurs in the latest law-code in the Old Testament. the so-called Priestly code. It was, therefore, possibly a late development. The daughters' freedom was just a little curtailed by a further ruling that in such cases they could not marry outside the family, so letting the land pass into the control of strangers (Num. 36: 1-12).

These are not small steps. Once women are included in both the demands and the protection of the law their status has been radically altered. Nor must one forget the influence attributed to women like Sarah, the ancestress of the faith. Miriam, the sister of Moses and Aaron was remembered as a prophetess (Exod. 15: 20) and the song of triumph attributed to her in the cultic procession of women after the Exodus has passed into the treasury of Old Testament devotional literature (Exod. 15: 21). Deborah was remembered as a prophetess whose energy and faith inspired Barak to lead the Israelites in victory over Sisera (Ju. 5).

Some women who were remembered as 'heroines of the faith' could display qualities that society has often labelled 'masculine'; there was, for example, Jael the wife of Heber, who drove a tentpeg through Sisera's skull with a few, deft strokes of a hammer. Heber may have had a treasure as a wife but she was no shy, shrinking or timid violet. We read of a prophetess in the time of Isaiah (Isa. 8: 3) and it was Huldah, the prophetess, whom Josiah consulted when the book of the law was found, and the oracle she returned him was as authoritative, crisp and direct as that attributed to any male prophet (II Ki. 22: 11-20). These must have been no isolated examples because Ezekiel can attack false prophetesses in general (Ezek. 13: 7-19. This attack was not of course because they were women, any more than the attack on male prophets earlier in the chapter, vv. 1-16, was because they were men. Both groups are attacked because of their false practices). Whatever the 'historicity' of some of these figures, tradition would not assign such roles to them if those roles were an entirely unknown phenomenon in ancient Israelite society.

Again, a story like that of Ruth, Naomi and Boaz shows that, in practice, women were often treated with a great deal of respect and with careful attention to their rights. Indeed, it illustrates how the law calling for protection for the widow, the immigrant, the orphan and the poor, could, and did, have an effect on the life of society. The same story shows how important the role of the woman was seen to be in perpetuating the line of a family's 'name'. The genealogy traces descent through the fathers, but the local women could rejoice that 'A son has been born to Naomi' (Ruth 4: 17). Certainly the genealogy which has been appended to the book identifies that child with Obed, none other than the grandfather of the great David.

The passage in praise of the good wife in Proverbs chapter 31 may arouse mixed reactions today. It is perhaps somewhat male-orientated!

> A good wife who can find?
> She is far more precious than jewels.
> The heart of her husband trusts in her,
> and he will have no lack of gain.
> She does him good, and not harm,
> all the days of her life. (vv. 10-12)

The question with which the passage opens does not mean it is near impossible to find such a wife, but rather that the search is well worth the effort. Allowing for the artificiality of the poem (it has been carefully constructed as a Hebrew acrostic, each line beginning with a successive letter of the alphabet) and for the somewhat male point of view, it nevertheless conveys a remarkable picture of the place and influence of the wife and mother in Hebrew society. She influences her husband and so his place in society:

> Her husband is known in the gates, when he sits among the elders of the land. (v. 23)

Her children owe her a debt they will come increasingly to realise:

> Her children rise up and call her blessed. (v. 28)

She helps the poor in society:

> She opens her hand to the poor
> and reaches out her hands to the needy. (v. 20)

She benefits the community at large:

> She opens her mouth with wisdom,
> and the teaching of kindness is on her tongue. (v. 26)

One feels that, in a different age and in a different culture, this woman would have been a company director, college Principal or even Prime Minister! What the picture does show is the importance of the family to Israelite society and of the woman's role both within and outside the home.

Male-dominated the society may have been, but Yahwism appears to have exerted a pressure which gradually moved towards the recognition that humankind, male and female, alike and together, form an 'image' of God, and each part of that totality has its due honour and its own particular contribution to make.

As we have seen, Yahweh can be spoken of as exercising both male and female roles in procreation. Occasionally, the female part is explicitly attributed to him. In answer to the lament of the exile community,

> But Zion said, 'The LORD has forsaken me,
> my LORD has forgotten me.' (Isa. 49: 14)

Isaiah of Babylon brings the assurance:

> Can a woman forget her sucking child,
> that she should have no compassion on the son of her womb?
> Even these may forget
> yet will I not forget you. (v. 15)

Not only is this a bold use of the metaphor of 'mother' for Yahweh, but the use of the Hebrew verb *rāham* in the phrase, '*that she should have no compassion*', raises an interesting point.[3] The verb *rāham* is derived from the noun *rehem* which means '*womb*'. We cannot assume that because this was its derivation, every time it was used the speaker had this connection consciously in mind. Nevertheless, it is not totally unconnected and its very frequent use of Yahweh's 'compassion' for his children is of interest. We must certainly note that the verb is not used exclusively of the female's concern for her children:

> As a father pities [Heb. *rāham*] his children,
> So the LORD pities those who fear him. (Ps. 103: 13)

Sometimes, however, the feminine side of the care seems to be to the fore. In Jeremiah 31: 15-20 Yahweh speaks of the sorrow in the land as being like that of a mother, Rachel, weeping for her lost children. A little later this is seen as a picture of God's concern for his children:

> Is Ephraim my dear son?
> Is he my darling child?
> For as often as I speak against him,
> I do remember him still.

> Therefore my heart yearns for him
> [lit. 'my bowels murmur']
> I will surely have mercy [Heb. *rāham*] on him,
> says the LORD. (31: 20)

With regard to the line 'my heart yearns for him', the literal rendering offered here lacks poetic elegance and delicacy in English. We have to remember that the viscera were thought to be the centre of emotions, just as in the English idiom it is the 'heart'. Whether we can follow Phyllis Trible and render these lines:

> Therefore my womb trembles for him
> I will truly show motherly compassion for him.[4]

is not certain. What can be said is that, at least, God as 'parent' combines the protective power and the tender love which brings together both paternal and maternal qualities.

It has sometimes been urged that the picture of God in Hosea chapter 11 (discussed in chapter 3, above) as the parent gently leading a small child in a walking harness, is more that of 'mother' than of 'father'. This may be so, although it is not made explicit; perhaps we should see this as another instance of Yahweh combining the roles of both parents. Sometimes Hosea 11: 9 is said to state explicitly that God is not 'male', since he says,

> I am God and not man.

Here the Hebrew word used, *'îsh*, is more often used for the 'male' as opposed to *'ādām* which can mean more generally 'human'. However, caution must be exercised. For we have a number of instances in the Old Testament where the two words can be paralleled, suggesting that a clear-cut distinction was not always by any means intended. One such example is found in Numbers 23: 19:

> God is not a man [*'îsh*], that he should lie, or a son of man [*ben 'ādām*], that he should repent.

Here both lines mean the same thing, 'God is not human'.[5] In the absence of any other explicit warrant, therefore, we may not build too much on Hosea 11: 9.

We have seen that, when Second Isaiah's hearers questioned the appropriateness of God's using such an instrument as the pagan Cyrus for his purpose, the prophet answers sharply:

> Woe to him who says to a father
> 'What are you begetting?'
> or to a woman, 'With what are you in travail?' (Isa. 45: 10)

To question Yahweh's authority carries the enormity of questioning *both* one's parents. God combines in his parental love the role of father and mother. Again, in a later chapter of Isaiah, we hear the assurance:

> As one whom his mother comforts,
> so I will comfort you;
> you shall be comforted in Jerusalem. (Isa. 66: 13)

So Yahweh combines the role of father and mother in his creation, or 'begetting' of his child, and also in the care and the love with which he leads and protects them. Yahweh has the fulness of being which comprehends both male and female in himself. That is surely why only a humanity that was both male and female could be said to be 'in his image'.

Just as we must be very careful about arguing from the etymology of a word to inference about what it meant to those who used it later in its life, so we must be careful about drawing deductions from the gender of a noun. In Hebrew, the word for 'spirit' (*rûah*) is more often feminine than masculine. That in itself tells us nothing, however. The distribution of nouns among genders in languages which possess them can be quite arbitrary. There is only one possible suggestion in the Old Testament that the 'spirit' of God might have a feminine role. Gen. 1: 2 could be translated as either 'a great wind was stirring the surface of the water' or 'the spirit of God was brooding (or 'hovering') over the waters'. The same Hebrew word means both 'wind' and 'spirit'. The phrase 'an X of God' is an idiomatic way of expressing a superlative. That is why it could be translated 'a great wind' (lit.

'a wind of God'). The verb used is very rare. It occurs elsewhere only in Deuteronomy 32: 11 where it speaks of an eagle 'hovering' or 'brooding' over its nest. The exact force of the verb is uncertain just because of the rarity of its use and that is why the English versions give it such a variety of renderings. It is therefore possible that Genesis 1:2 likens God's spirit to a mother bird brooding over her nest with its eggs to give them life. It is uncertain, however, and it has to be said that the thought is nowhere else developed in the Old Testament and so cannot be pressed into service here.

It is quite different with the concept of 'Wisdom' (Heb. *hokmah*), not because it is a feminine noun, but because Wisdom is personified as a woman in Proverbs chapter 8 and in Ecclesiasticus (The Wisdom of Ben Sirach) chapter 24.

In the opening chapters of the Book of Proverbs, 'Folly' is portrayed as a woman of loose morals who seeks to entice young men into her house. She is like a prostitute offering pleasure which, however, turns out to be a trap of misery and ruin.

> She sits at the door of her house . . .
> calling to those who pass by . . .
> 'Whoever is simple, let him turn in here!' . . .
> But he does not know that the dead are there,
> that her guests are in the depths of Sheol. (Prov. 9: 14-18)

By contrast, Wisdom is also personified as a woman who invites all to her 'house':

> Wisdom has built her house,
> she has set up her seven pillars . . .
> She has sent out her maids to call
> from the highest places in the town,
> 'Whoever is simple, let him turn in here!'
> To him who is without sense she says,
> 'Come, eat of my bread
> and drink of the wine I have mixed.
> Leave simpleness, and live,
> and walk in the way of insight.' (Prov. 9: 1-6)

Wisdom cries out in the streets, calling on all who will to learn of her.

> How long, O simple ones, will you love being simple?
> ... Give heed to my reproof;
> behold, I will pour out my thoughts to you;
> I will make my words known to you. (Prov. 1: 22f.)

Her teaching offers greater rewards than money. She it is who gives insight to kings to rule and govern justly, and all who follow her find life (8: 35). Indeed, she has unique credentials as a teacher. She was the first-born of all creation (8: 22-31), so that all creation is stamped with her character. To follow her is to observe that there is a moral 'grain' to the universe and to discover the secret of true life. To follow her precepts is to go with this grain in the universe rather than rub up against it, for it is essentially a *moral* grain. There is a moral order at the heart of all creation and Wisdom leads people to it. This is how the world is. That is why it works as it does. Hence, to follow and obey Lady Wisdom is to know the life that prospers and succeeds. Wisdom, indeed, was not only the first-born of all creation, but actively assisted God in his creation (8: 27-31).

> And now, my sons, listen to me:
> happy are those who keep my ways.
> Hear instruction and be wise,
> and do not neglect it.
> Happy is the man who listens to me,
> watching daily at my gates,
> waiting beside my doors.
> For he who finds me finds life,
> and obtains favour from the LORD;
> but he who misses me injures himself;
> all who love me hate death. (8: 32-36)

It is not entirely surprising that Wisdom should appear as a woman. There was clearly some influence from Egyptian Wisdom literature on Israel, and in Egypt, the figure of wisdom, *Maat*, was a goddess. In the Hebrew Scriptures, however, she is not that. She is hardly even an 'hypostasis', that is, a personality separate and distinct from God. She is rather a personification of God himself. It is a highly dramatic and metaphorical way of saying that wisdom is a fundamental attribute of God's own nature. The figure is a graphic expression of the theological truth that God has implanted a general revelation of himself in the natural order of the created world and in human experience. How significant it is that such an 'extension of Yahweh's personality' should be depicted in feminine terms. Her gentle invitation to all to come home and be nourished and taught by her, and her influence for good on all who belong to her 'family', make her just like the virtuous woman of Proverbs chapter 31. Further, her training expresses her care and concern for all who are wandering, and her ability to express truth so that the 'simple' can understand it is like a mother gently and patiently teaching her children; this represents characteristics which have proved vital to every generation and which have always been associated primarily with the role of motherhood.

It is as though, amidst all the strongly male dominated talk of God and images of him, the 'female' part of him had to break through. For humankind in their maleness and femaleness have that in them which responds to the feminine. Perhaps there is something of an analogy here to the place which Mary, the mother of Jesus, attained in Christian devotion in the strongly male dominated tradition of western Christendom.

We need not, then, rush to the opposite extreme of declaring that God is, after all, simply female. We can recognise the male-dominated talk of God in the Old Testament, without insisting that therefore exclusive maleness is of the essence of the Deity. Nor need we fly from sexual images altogether to claim that God is a kind of divine neuter. The Old Testament at least points the way to saying that God is both male and female, and as such offers wholeness to a humanity created in his image just because it was created male and female.

NOTES TO CHAPTER TEN

1. There is a large and growing literature on the subject. Among the best known are the writings of Phyllis Trible. See 'God, Nature of in the Old Testament', *Interpreter's Dictionary of the Bible, Supp. Vol.*, Abingdon, Nashville, 1976, pp. 368f.; *God and the Rhetoric of Sexuality*, Philadelphia, 1978; 'Depatriarchalizing God in Biblical Interpretation', *Journal of the American Academy of Religion*, 41, 1973, pp. 30-48. For a critique of this, see J.W. Miller, 'Depatriarchalizing God in Biblical Tradition: A Critique', *Catholic Biblical Quarterly*, 48, 1986, pp. 609-616. See also J.H. Otwell, *And Sarah Laughed: The Status of Women in the Old Testament*, Philadelphia, 1977; Leonard Swidler, *Biblical Affirmation of Women*, Philadelphia, 1979; R. Hamerton Kelly, *God the Father*, Philadelphia, 1979; Virginia Mollenkott, *The Divine Feminine: The Biblical Imagery of God as Female*, New York, 1983. A whole issue of *The Journal for the Study of the Old Testament*, (22, Sheffield, 1982), was devoted to the influence of Women's Studies on Biblical Studies.

2. Yet, even so, we must note that it is the *masculine* singular participle (*Po'lel*) of the verb which is used.

3. The issue here is unaffected by our choice in pointing this as a participle or taking it as an infinitive with the preposition before it. Nor does it matter that the form is masculine. It obviously implies that God is 'mother-like' in his compassion. It does not imply that he *is* a mother.

4. Possibly Phyllis Trible in her book, The *Rhetoric of Sexuality*, can be charged with making too much of the alleged etymological derivation of this verb.

5. See also, Gen. 32: 28-29, Pss. 49: 2-3, 62: 9-10.

CONCLUSION

We have walked round the picture gallery in which these, and many other, Old Testament pictures of God are displayed. When we visit any picture gallery we see pictures which bear the signs of the age and idiom in which they were painted, so that we can speak of 'the Dutch School of the 16th. century' or 'English 19th. century water colour landscapes'. Even if these styles are not the way in which artists would paint now, they still speak to us because we can sense the integrity of the artist and enter into the way he or she saw the subject and felt about it. For the same reason we can appreciate and be enriched by pictures, or music, which convey deep religious faith and sensitivities, even if we ourselves do not share the particular religious tradition of the artist or composer. Any glimpse of the great realities of human life and any profound emotion can lay hold of us and enlarge our own horizons.

Some of these Old Testament pictures of God may well strike us as strange. Sometimes we would rather use different pictures, even when we want to say the same kind of things about the God of our faith. To use the simile we have employed more than once, some old pictures need cleaning and restoring before we can appreciate them fully, and even when we see them as the artist intended them to be, there may have to be a process of re-interpretation before we can really hear what they have to say to us.

Nevertheless, the deep faith and religious adoration which lay behind these pictures means that they still have power to evoke a response today. They have nourished and sustained the faith and worship of Jewish religious communities across all their chequered history, in persecution in medieval ghettoes as well as in twentieth century concentration camps. They have inspired and maintained the hope and determination to build again the land promised to their forefathers, and have helped to keep alight the flame of a vision which many hostile winds have never quite managed to extinguish.

For Christians the pictures have found a new lease of life as they have been taken up in the New Testament. Indeed, it would be the subject of another whole study to go on to ask just how all these images have found their place there, subtly changed but nevertheless enhanced and used anew to throw light on the person and mission of Jesus Christ. Just as he sees his life as the new wine which bursts the old wineskins (Mark 2: 22), so he embodies, but also transforms, earlier conceptions of God. And yet the newness of his revelation of God would be far less comprehensible if we did not share his own sense of roots in the Hebrew Scriptures, the Old Testament for Christians.

It is because of this that preaching about the God who is so richly portrayed in these and other pictures is both possible and worthwhile. We have seen how behind each of the pictures as they are so variously shown to us there is a long tradition of expounding, re-interpreting and re-applying them in new situations. This is true within the Old Testament itself and it is true in the way that New Testament writers have found new vitality within them. This suggests that they have the quality of being always contemporary, possessing an inner life which has the power to speak to ever-new generations across the divide of the ages and of differing cultures. As the basis for preaching today they may therefore help close the 'credibility gap' between God and our own generation.

So for both Jews and Christians, to return to these pictures of God is to return again to the spring whose waters nourish and sustain, and may even have the power to awaken, our faith.

INDEX

Abraham 47, 54, 58, 59, 66, 71, 134-136, 141
Amarna Letters 54, 59
Amos 20, 58, 70, 78, 82, 84, 127, 169, 170, 174
analogy 1, 3, 15, 190, 202
anointed (see 'Messiah')
anthropomorphism 3, 6, 34, 76, 83
apocalyptic 10
Ark of the Covenant 83, 160-163, 166
Arnold, M. 142
Avenger of Blood 21-23

Book of the Covenant 72
Brandon, S.G.F. 74
Buber, M. 121

Caird, G.B. 3, 15
Carroll, L. 14
Childs, B.S. 16
chaos 106, 108-109, 117, 120, 122, 164, 170, 191
Chronicles 105, 119, 124
cities of refuge 23
council of heaven 70, 74, 85, 86, 191
covenant 41, 58-60, 62-64, 68, 69, 72, 76,
                                82, 83, 110, 115, 145, 160, 163,
                                166, 178, 181, 182, 190
Crenshaw, J.L. 73
Cyrus 42, 57

Daniel 18, 74, 117-118
David 10, 22, 23, 46, 62, 63, 97-99,
                                102, 105, 106, 115, 119, 125-129, 142-146,

	152, 161, 162, 166, 168, 176, 179, 195
Davidson, R.	142
Day, J.	122
Day of Yahweh	169
Deuteronomists	10, 40, 44, 60, 77, 98, 101, 102, 163, 165, 166
Deuteronomy	2, 10, 11, 18, 20, 21, 23, 26, 44, 45, 47, 51, 60, 62, 67, 70, 71, 73, 78, 81, 82, 98, 101, 121, 125, 136, 156, 165, 170, 173, 182, 192, 193, 194, 200
Driver, G.R.	73
Dunn, J.	16
El	53, 54
Exodus	2, 17, 24-26, 32, 44, 47, 50, 54, 67, 68, 72, 84, 105, 121, 145, 156, 159, 160, 164, 178, 180, 181, 194
Exodus from Egypt	25-27, 65, 159-160
Ezekiel	32, 72, 77, 79, 102, 115, 147, 152, 174, 184, 195
Fall, the	5
Goldingay, J.	16
Habiru	54
Hosea	54, 64, 65, 86, 88, 101, 121, 168, 175, 177-180, 181-185, 187, 198, 199
Isaiah	10, 14, 16, 24-27, 29, 36-39, 41-43, 47, 49, 57-58, 66, 69, 71-72, 76, 79-81, 84, 87-89, 96, 102, 103, 107, 114-117, 122, 125, 129, 132, 137-139, 142, 144, 151, 156, 161, 167, 168, 170-172, 174, 185, 186, 189, 195, 197, 199
Isaiah of Jerusalem (Isa 1-39)	16, 144, 167

Jeremiah 10, 15, 19, 27, 32, 38, 40, 44,
52, 61, 65, 67-68, 71, 85, 86, 126,
127, 132, 135, 141-144, 147-152,
163, 170, 174, 178, 183, 184, 197
Jerusalem (see 'Zion') 16, 26, 29, 30, 37, 39, 40-42, 49,
51, 59, 62, 79, 83, 99, 100, 103,
106, 107, 113, 115, 116, 121, 127,
135, 136, 138, 139, 143, 144, 162,
163, 166, 167, 171, 172, 184, 186, 199
Job 10, 28, 49, 86, 132-134
Joel 10, 137, 138
Johnson, A.R. 122, 142, 155, 157

Kelly, R.H. 203

Lemche, N. 173
Levirate marriage 20, 21, 51
Lord of Hosts 14, 27, 38, 113, 114, 117, 121,
132, 145, 160-163, 172

Macquarrie. J. 2, 4, 6, 7, 14
Malachi 58, 67, 136
Mays, J.L. 187
Messiah ('anointed') 28, 42, 57, 62, 99, 113, 144
metaphor 2, 3, 5, 6, 15, 32, 61,
106, 132, 180, 191, 197
Miller, J.W. 203
Mollenkott, V.. 203

Nielsen, K. 142
Noah 58
North, C.R. 14

Otwell, J.H. 203

Philistines 73, 81, 98, 162, 181
Phillips, A.J. 30
Priestly Writer 4, 16, 20, 22, 58, 76, 190, 191, 194
Pritchard, J.B. 121, 156, 174

prophetic symbolism 39, 179
Psalms 6, 10, 27, 29, 35-38, 62, 69-71, 75
                  76, 78-83, 99-100, 104-113, 117, 120,
                     122, 123, 125, 131, 137, 140-143, 146,
                 153-155, 162-165, 168, 190, 192, 197, 203

Ruth 21, 30, 51, 73, 195

Satan 86
Second Isaiah (Isa. 40-55) 14, 26-27, 42, 47, 57, 58, 71,
                         76, 80-81, 84, 87-89, 102, 107,
                            115, 132, 137, 142, 144, 151,
                                 156, 161, 185, 189, 199
simile 2-4, 15, 205
Snaith, N.H. 28, 30
Swidler, S.L. 203
symbol 3, 6, 15, 80, 161, 191

Tanak 2, 14
Tribble, P. 198, 203
Trito-Isaiah (Isa. 56-66) 41, 66, 80, 88, 138, 170, 171, 185

Ugaritic 73, 95, 121, 165

Vaux, R. de 46, 73

Weippert, M. 173
Whitelam, K.C. 121
Whybray, R.N. 74
Wisdom 10, 41-43, 47, 61, 73, 78, 121,
                              128, 129, 169, 196, 200-202
Wisdom writers 10, 47, 73

Yahwist 35, 58

Zion 29, 40-41, 62-63, 110, 113, 115-117,
                     127, 138, 143, 150, 162, 163, 166, 168,
                                      170, 185-186, 197